# THE CHOSEN
# AND
# THE CHOICE

Jean-Jacques Servan-Schreiber has had an impressive career in journalism and politics, ranging from editorial writer for *Le Monde*, to Special assistant to Prime Minister Mendès France, to the founder of *L'Express* in 1953. After serving in Algeria in 1956 he wrote *Lieutenant en Algérie*, followed by *Le Défi Americain*, alerting Europe to new developments in technology and education. He was elected member of Parliament, president of the region of Lorraine (1970–78) and in 1980 published *Le Défi mondial*. After working as President of the Centre of Computer-literacy, created by French President Mitterrand he embarked on his current job presiding over the International Committee of Carnegie-Mellon University, the world leader in computing science applied to education.

Also by Jean-Jacques Servan-Schreiber:

LIEUTENANT EN ALGÉRIE, Julliard, 1957.

LE DÉFI AMÉRICAIN, Denoël, 1967.

LE MANIFESTE RADICAL, Denoël, 1970.

LE POUVOIR RÉGIONAL, Grasset, 1972.

LE DÉFI MONDIAL, Fayard, 1980.

KNOWLEDGE REVOLUTION, CMU Press, 1986.

JEAN-JACQUES SERVAN-SCHREIBER
with David Krivine

# THE CHOSEN
# AND
# THE CHOICE

FUTURA

# CONTENTS

1. Israel in danger. . . . . . . . . . . . . . . . . . . . 7
2. "The world has become Jewish". . . . . 25
3. The leadership question. . . . . . . . . . . . 53
4. Explosion of a generation . . . . . . . . . . 67
5. A new kind of hero . . . . . . . . . . . . . . 79
6. The land of tomorrow . . . . . . . . . . . . 101
7. Make the desert bloom . . . . . . . . . . 123
8. Lack of vision, not of talent . . . . . . . 137
9. "But sir, that's his name!". . . . . . . . . 151
10. Pessimists are more serious . . . . . . . . 171
11. The choice . . . . . . . . . . . . . . . . . . . . 191

ANNEXES

*Partition Plan, 211.—Declaration of Independence, 215.—Palestine National Convention, 219.—Resolutions 242 and 338, 225.—Camp David, 227.—The World Jewish Population, 236.*

5

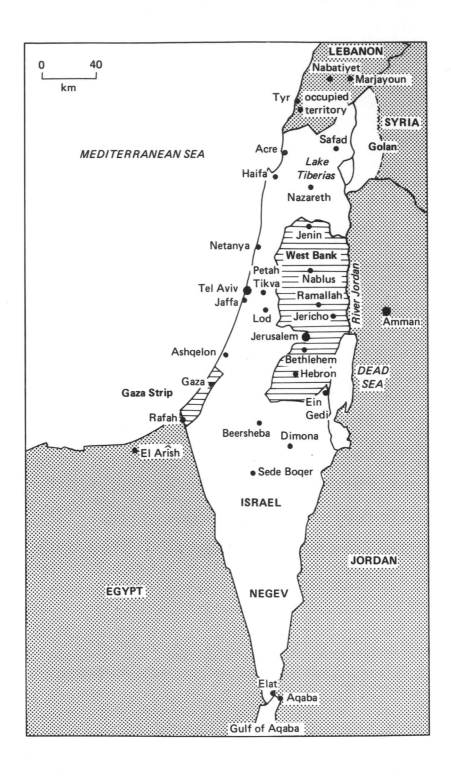

# 1

# Israel in danger

Israelis never foresaw how the maintenance of their rule over Palestinian-inhabited regions would erode the abilities of their own army. As happened to the French in Algeria, and to the Americans in Vietnam.

Tsahal's pilots and tank commanders have evoked the world's admiration. Relegated to the role of policemen and ordered to clout stone-throwing adolescents, their image has changed and they are painfully aware of it. The result is a loss of faith in their own task and purpose; they begin to question the patriotic aims they are supposed to serve.

The present leaders in Israel do not heed these warning signs. Their minds are made up and they will not change—any more than Robert McNamara and Lyndon Johnson would change 25 years ago. The Pentagon had started sending "military advisers" to South Vietnam. The French tragedy in that country should have been a warning, Washington's

politicians ignored it. They failed to foresee
the American tragedy that would ensue, as I
can testify

*       *       *

I was then again in uniform. I had been
mobilized to serve in South Algeria by a
government eager to terminate, at least for a
time, my newspaper articles attacking their
policies. Nevertheless a letter reached me
from a certain American senator enclosing the
text of a speech he had made criticizing
severely the French Algerian campaign.

It was a lucid attack on the whole principle
of colonialism and a prediction of its ruinous
aftermath. I sent a copy to the periodical with
which I was associated, *L'Express*, in Paris,
asking for its publication together with a
photograph of this still unknown senator.
John Kennedy appeared for the first time on
the cover of a news magazine. He did not
forget it.

Our contacts were maintained after his election to the presidency. During a respite (following the Bay of Pigs mishap and the Cuban
missile crisis) he invited me to call on him at
the White House. This was at the beginning of
1963.

## Israel in danger

Seated on his legendary rocking-chair he
listed five subjects in the field of world affairs.
He asked me which of them I would like to
discuss and in what order. They were: the
European union, nuclear defence, the techni-
cal revolution (still at its beginnings), America's economic relations with the outside world
and, not least, decolonization.

I asked his forgiveness for answering
bluntly. "In my eyes," I said, "none of these
topics has immediate urgency. The one I want
to discuss with you does not figure on your
list...." After a short silence: "It is Vietnam."

Astonished, Kennedy thought he had heard
me wrong. "Vietnam? But that is a local
matter," he said, "we are concerned with it
only indirectly. The French have asked me to
help the liberal regime of Saigon, as we do in
twenty places on the globe. We don't have to
do more than that. I'm sure the Vietnamese are
able to look after themselves.

"As far as I'm concerned," he went on,
"there are other things to worry about. Russia's nuclear capacity is a menace. We have still
to build up our relations with Europe. Inside
the States the problem of the blacks has
become threatening. Most perplexing of all is
the need to rescue the Third World from stark

poverty; about which I'm far from optimistic. These are the issues engrossing my attention; I never expected you to add the one you did."

"I can only repeat," I insisted, "Vietnam has to be the first preoccupation. Your great country will get drawn into the conflict. You may not see that now, but it is going to happen: it can't be avoided. The military, zealous for victory and galvanized by the professional patriots, will before long turn this situation into a tragedy.

"Let me tell you about a senior French army officer who tried to find out why we were defeated in Vietnam. He was given access to the files in Hanoi. His research took several years. He summarized it in an objective, factual account entitled quite simply 'Dien Bien Phu'. The name of the author is Jules Roy.

"You won't have time to read all 700 pages in the original French, why don't you have someone condense it in English to 30 pages? This analysis will convince you. If you start campaigning against Ho Chi Minh and General Giap, you will fall into the same trap."

Kennedy pressed a button on his desk and asked Mrs Jacqueline Kennedy, whose French is excellent, to step in. She obligingly undertook to read the book and make a précis for her husband.

The president did not stop at that. He suggested I have a word with the Defense Secretary, and arranged a meeting for me. I breakfasted with McNamara the following morning. He listened carefully to what I had to say, then cut short.

"Listen," he said, "there are a number of differences between the French position in Vietnam and our position if we come into the war. Chief of them is: *the helicopters.* We shall deploy them on such a scale that the Vietminh guerillas will be pinned to the ground. Saigon's land forces will do the job while we protect them from above. I understand that Dien Bien Phu has left a bitter memory with you French; but this misfortune will not recur. We have the *helicopters....*"

Back in my hotel I sought, at the risk of being dubbed obsessive, a second interview with the president. Received again at the White House I explained to him that McNamara had got it wrong. I stressed that his miscalculation could have grave consequences.

Kennedy decided he would like to have the views of his brother Robert, and fixed an appointment for me at the Justice Department. Quick-thinking and responsive, the younger Kennedy told me he would take the matter up. He would speak to the president about it when the opportunity arose.

By the time the opportunity arose in 1965 John Kennedy was no longer alive. The US army had entered the field and the nation's honour was at stake. The new president Lyndon Johnson relished the role of warlord. He excluded Robert Kennedy and other moderate elements from his inner councils. America had fallen into the trap of military adventure—just when the country was coming to grips with the new knowledge revolution that carries the future. The Vietnam war got into its destructive stride as, in the technological field, the "American challenge" was reaching its peak.

*       *       *

The practice of domination, essentially non-democratic, has become more baneful to the Israeli occupant than he cares to admit. We who have gone through the colonial experience in our own countries recognize the symptoms: confused values, uncertainties, excessive hubris. A minority in Israel reacts aggressively; others feel anxious over errors committed and have misgivings about the future.

The retention of Greater Israel including the occupied areas presents demographic problems which could threaten the Jewishness of the Jewish state. A decade from now Arabs will account for almost half (45 per cent) of the population. The two ethnic groups have different beliefs and loyalties. The discord between their conflicting aspirations may sweep away the Zionist dream.

In the West Bank (the zone that Israel's first right-wing prime minister, Menahem Begin, made a political issue of renaming Judaea and Samaria), 90 per cent of the inhabitants are Palestinians; and in the Gaza Strip 98 per cent.

These populations are growing through natural increase; is it conceivable that Jews should settle in sufficient numbers to outpace them? Early in 1988 premier Yitzhak Shamir planted trees ceremoniously in Samaria, inviting his fellow-citizens to make their home there; this only days after clashes between Arab inhabitants and Jewish colonists had left many wounded.

The lethal war between Iraq and Iran has for the last seven years kept both countries away from the anti-Zionist front. But hostilities in the Gulf fading away who knows what crusade the weakened but nevertheless still highly-armed Iraqis may not then unleash on the Israelis?

Egypt, previously Israel's most powerful antagonist, has its own insecurities. A population explosion frustrates all economic aid programmes. Islamic pressures threaten Cairo's moderate policies. Poverty and fundamentalism together make an unstable brew, as is manifest in Khumeini's Persia. Continued violence throughout the occupied territories could inflame the Egyptian mob, putting at risk the formal treaty now keeping the two rival states at peace.

Could the Palestinians' "Arab brethren" keep their eyes averted for ever? The Arab coalition that engineered three of the five wars in which Israel was engaged may sooner or later be revived. This time the forces they dispose of will be more substantial. The Arab powers have available on her borders 7,000 tanks, 3,000 modern artillery pieces, a thousand fighter planes, 200 helicopters and at least fifty missile ramps within range of Israel's principal cities. An estimate by her army authorities predicts as casualties on their side in any new hostilities 7,000 dead and 20,000 wounded.

These figures were tabled for examination before experts, civil and military, gathered at a seminar of the Van Leer Institute in Jerusalem. The following conclusions were reached:

Unless something is done to change the status quo the present unrest could develop into a civil war.

A suggested solution is to abandon the bulk of the occupied territories, while ensuring the necessary security precautions. Israel would then remain a homogeneous nation. By the year 2000, Jewish inhabitants within Israel proper will amount to 80 per cent of the population.

Thirdly, the country's energies, now wasted on the struggle against the Palestinians, could be channelled constructively in the two zones which remain under-populated and under-developed inside Israel's own borders: the Galilee and the Negev.

The country's security to-date depends less on the holding of this or that frontier than on the maintenance of a qualitative military edge. Technology and training together create an impressive capacity, demonstrated in the destruction during the Lebanese war of all Soviet missiles in the Beka Valley. By concentrating all her resources Israel has ensured her defence in the past. She will go on ensuring it in the present, but confidence about that in Jerusalem is not as great as it was.

The race for excellence—here like everywhere else, as both the Americans and the Russians can testify—is becoming ruinous. Israel cannot bank on continued multi-billion American aid year after year. Nor has she managed to emulate the Japanese in building up an export surplus sufficient to pay for all her import needs, arms included. When resources, human and financial, are diverted on a large scale, economic development suffers.

My mind has always been haunted by the ills of colonialism. After this malady had bled the Europeans dry, it began to infect the US, home of the man who had been a champion of anti-colonialism, F. D. Roosevelt.

I now warn Israelis of the perils that lay ahead for them, but they reject the comparison. As they see it, their problem is different. Just as the bitter French experience was no precedent for the Americans, so the failure of America's efforts to clamp law and order on Vietnam provides no precedent for the Israelis.

## Israel in danger

The French themselves had not heeded warnings from their own past or the past of other colonial powers, despite exhortations given repeatedly by Prime Minister Mendes-France. For seven long years he declaimed from the parliamentary rostrum against the loss of young lives and the waste of treasure caused by the hopeless Indo-Chinese involvement.

That war ended in 1954. During the same year Ahmed Ben-Bella launched his insurrection against the French in Algeria. Though admitting that Mendes-France had been right about Vietnam, the French rejected his bid for peace in North Africa. He was replaced in 1955 by socialist leader Guy Mollet, who chose in this way to demonstrate his "patriotism". ("He at least isn't a Jew," observed Jacques Duclos, head of the Communists in the National Assembly, who voted for Mollet's appointment.) The French army was transported to Algeria for a further seven blood-soaked years, failing there as it had failed in South-East Asia.

It was in this spasm of colonialist activity that the Suez expedition was thought up. Prepared by France and Britain in secret, it required Israel's participation. The intention

CC-B

17

was to destroy Egypt's dictator Abdul Nasser. His nationalization of the Suez Canal had made him a folk-hero in the Arab world. The two European powers needed military help on the ground. While they parachuted troops over the canal area, Israel would invade Sinai.

This eccentric exploit did give Israel legitimate gains: an end to terrorist raids from Gaza and to the blockade of Israel's southern coast at the Tiran Straits. Long-term results were less felicitous. The Jewish state found itself for the first time siding with the old colonial powers against a resurgent Arab nationalism. Ben-Gurion sensed this was wrong. He hesitated long before joining in, as is revealed in his diaries kept in the desert at Sde Boker.

Jews view themselves as battling for the right to a national home in Eretz-Israel, a territory which extends from the Mediterranean to the Jordan river. The area, small though it is, accommodates a resident population of Arabs who do not want to live under foreign rule. Israel's insistence on maintaining that rule—pending peace negotiations which never seem to eventuate—has led to a new clash, this time within the zones Israel controls.

## Israel in danger

The clash is both ethnic, between Jews and Arabs, and geographic, between residents within the pre-1967 borders and residents of the West Bank and Gaza. Consequently, despite evident differences with Europe's former suzereinty over distant territories, the confrontation with Israel has colonialist overtones.

Voices used to be raised in Europe against the imperialistic propensity for dominion over others. Six hundred Israeli scholars and scientists appealed to the press and public for a stop to dominion over the Arabs. Needed is not solutions imposed from above by an international conference but a decision by both sides to talk. The world community can create the framework for direct negotiations, provided the essential end-purpose is kept in view: the conclusion of an agreement between Israelis and Palestinians.

In a statement entitled "Put an End to Occupation" the six hundred academicians declared: "There is no solution to the situation in which Israel is caught, as long as the rule it imposes on Arab inhabitants of the territories continues.... The use of power to enforce law and order is a way of ignoring the roots of the problem. Burdening the army with the task of policing the territories prevents it from carrying out its main duty: the defence of the country.

"We cannot accept that young conscripts find themselves compelled to open fire on youths and civilians, because of the government's unwillingness to deal with the source of the problem. This situation is unacceptable morally and diplomatically. We call on the government to take steps immediately that will lead to negotiations, before they lose control of the situation."

Supporters of the petition include personalities whose signature cannot be overlooked, men like Don Patinkin, former president of the Hebrew University, Shmuel Eisenstadt, sociologist of world repute, historian Shmuel Ettinger, economist Menahem Ya'ari, writer Amos Oz. Sponsor of the initiative, law professor Mordechai Kremnitzer, says that response flooded in from all the country's universities—in Jerusalem, Tel Aviv, Haifa, Rehovot and Beersheba.

Comparable approaches years ago from men of letters in the US demanding peace talks in Vietnam infuriated President Johnson and his ministers, who saw these spokesmen as "saboteurs of the American presence in the outside world". Labelled allies of the enemy, the anti-war lobby was considered more dangerous than the Vietminh guerillas. The crusading fervour that overtook the US divided the population between the "hawks" who called for a fight to the finish and the "doves" who wanted peace at any price.

Student riots and police repression, climaxed at the Democratic Party convention in Chicago in 1968, brought the outburst of civil strife onto every television screen. Americans discovered that the war was not confined to the battlefield in Vietnam, it had penetrated into their own living-rooms. There is nothing new in that. Time and again the colonialist dilemma divides the best spirits, causing civil turmoil. The ordeal was undergone by the French and then by the Americans, is it to be played out afresh by the Israelis?

Only they can decide. Mark Goldberg, head of Project Renewal in the Negev city Dimona, made a statement using as his headline the title of Barbara Tuchman's book *March of Folly*. He writes:

"The volume was published (in Britain) in 1984, at a time when Israelis were attempting to come to grips with their previous government's own example of folly: the Lebanese war. This was the first time we had entered hostilities out of choice and for a motive other than survival.... All the major political parties and leaders in Israel and the Diaspora conspired to pretend: that the war was defensive (it was called 'Peace in Galilee'); that it was inevitable because of terrorist activities; and that its aims were limited to 'clearing an area 40 kms. into Lebanon'....

"Despite warnings of the disaster that lay in wait for Israel, the war proceeded, ending up in a sordid retreat. Even that required a change of government. The cost to Israel was many hundreds of dead and wounded; economic damage exceeding $6b.; a damaged national consensus and international image; a prime minister devastated by the enormity of what he had been duped into authorizing; a defence minister humiliated and dismissed from office by a judicial commission forced on the government by massive public demonstrations.

"In that perspective the events of the last seven weeks can be seen as inevitable: violence born out of hopelessness on one side and lack of options on the other. It is the hubris and nemesis of a Greek tragedy. All the characteristics listed by Barbara Tuchman are there: rigidity of thinking, refusal to examine alternatives; a disregard of negative signs."

Ze'ev Schiff, veteran military correspondent, let off steam in the daily paper he works for, *Ha'Aretz*: "How did our army handle the Palestinian uprising? Lamentably. The powerful military force that we have bred over the last forty years, with its thousands of tanks and warplanes, became a giant with feet of clay when faced with rebellious Palestinian youngsters in the streets. This contest has inscribed the most lugubrious chapter in our military annals. The upshot is self-evident: we have to negotiate with the Palestinians, period."

*       *       *

Pressures from abroad, words of censure, criticisms from the Jewish community in the US—who have pride of place in any discussion of Israel's problems—all serve no purpose. The answer can only be found inside the country.

Shimon Peres believes (as I have learnt from the long weeks we spent together) that he must find a way of tying up the two ends. Israelis must be persuaded to make the sacrifice of agreeing to a territorial compromise. In order to do that, they (and particularly the young among them) must have before their eyes a new ideal to replace the old—an alternative grand design, creative enough to absorb their future energies and enthusiasm.

The challenge is to restore the spirit that brought Israel into existence forty years ago on the ashes of the Holocaust. Zionists must gird their loins afresh. Is it too much to ask? Yet Jews are not accustomed to resting on their laurels. They have learned from hard experience that nothing can be taken for granted, nothing left to chance. Efforts must be perpetually renewed, otherwise the game is lost.

The past cannot be preserved intact, some of it has to be discarded. Looking back is unrewarding. The scene is littered with nationalistic prejudices, disputes over borders, acts of repression. The future offers brighter prospects. The task ahead is to regain Israel's position as a leading nation in the "knowledge economy" of our new world. There lies her salvation. That is where all eyes should turn.

## 2

# "The world has become Jewish"

His face had been weary the evening before, at the end of a long stint including his weekly meeting with the prime minister and the minister of defence. A few hours' sleep was enough however, he was fresh at dawn when we met again.

His apartment, on the ground floor in Jabotinsky Street, is small but functional. We sit in the living-room. Repeatedly the phone rings, cutting into our talk. He answers it himself. Half the calls are from abroad—New York, London, Paris, Bonn, Washington. He is not bothered by the interruptions, he likes this moment-to-moment contact with the outside world.

He has held high positions for a long time, since in fact the state was founded. Ben-Gurion chose two young activists, still in their thirties, as his right-hand men in the military field. One was Moshe Dayan, appointed chief-of-staff, the other Shimon Peres—my host this morning—who took over as director-general of the Defence Ministry.

Peres achieved Cabinet post before long, and rose eventually to be prime minister in 1984, heading an alliance of Labour and Likud. In 1986 Vice-Premier Yitzhak Shamir of Likud replaced him, in accordance with the coalition agreement. Peres became vice-premier in his turn, taking over also the foreign ministry from Shamir.

"I want to change the subject of our discussion today," I told him. "Something new has cropped up and, quite frankly, I'm apprehensive."

He knew what I was talking about: the uprising, sudden and forceful, of a new Palestinian generation, boys and girls aged 15 to 20. Beginning last December in the inferno of the Gaza Strip it sprouted through the West Bank, occupied for the last twenty years. It came with lightning speed. The government and army of Israel had never seen anything like this. In Ramallah, Nablus, Bethlehem and Hebron, Palestinian youths born under the occupation moved to open insurrection, throwing stones and petrol bombs, burning cars, closing schools, planting their national flag. The troubles had spread inside Israel, extending as far north as Nazareth in the Galilee.

They held up streets in the face of army jeeps. The first deaths drove the flame of unrest further to every small town and village. These unarmed rebels captured the world's attention, through the numerous lenses of press, radio and television. They challenged the conscience of Israel.

In the Knesset, sitting at the government bench, Shimon Peres shed the diplomatic tone usual to a foreign minister. "What logic, what morals, what historic wisdom," he declaimed, "orders us to fire at a young girl in the court-yard of a school? Are we assuring the security of Israel in this manner? What have we to gain by occupying 360 square kilometres of Gaza, populated by more than half-a-million hostile Arabs?"

He called for a peace dialogue with the enemy. Defence Minister Yitzhak Rabin, his colleague in the Labour Party: "The first necessity is to restore law and order. Once calm is restored we may discover that there are partners to negotiate with."

The familiar historic trap. When rebellion develops, negotiation looks like appeasement. When law and order are brought back for a spell, there is no longer any pressing need to negotiate. And so on, until it is too late and reason ceases to prevail.

I had gone through the same scenario of illusion and tragedy not long ago in both my motherlands: in France over Algeria, in the United States over Vietnam.

I meet his glance and speak candidly:

"It may be that you should free yourself from your present ministerial duties, and concentrate on delivering a new message of hope. Perhaps you ought to spend some time in isolation. It is hard to see how you can preserve your integrity, indeed your very identity as long as you remain involved in the daily actions of this government. And if you lose your identity, everything may be lost.

"I don't talk about world opinion. We know it condemns Israel everywhere, and sometimes very harshly. I talk about your own people. Soon they will have to decide their fate. The elections this time are crucial. If you obscure the voters' perception by being associated too long with policies of which you disapprove, they may ballot for the demagogues. There is still time to keep the options open, but for how long?"

"My impression is the same," he replies.

## *"The world has become Jewish"*

"We keep asking ourselves in the Labour movement whether the time has not come for the whole party to resign from the governing coalition. Where can we do our duty best— inside or outside the Cabinet? One thing I am sure about, that Labour's resignation would deal a serious blow to the cause of peace."

He knows his history: the forty centuries of the Jewish people; the forty years of Israel; the colonial wars fought during those same forty years of France and the US. He is also familiar with the potential of the Palestinians, those "Jews of the Arab world", even though he hardly ever mentions them. He had a close relationship with Moshe Dayan, who spoke Arabic. The historic victor of the Six Day War used to stroll in civilian clothes, unarmed and without bodyguard, in occupied Arab towns. He talked with the Palestinians, sensing their pride, their solidarity.

"When you speak from the podium, your conviction comes across; but what echo do you expect from the wider Israeli public, under the shock of the present troubles?"

"What worries me about public opinion," Peres rejoins, "is that simple and practical problems get transformed into ideological issues; and then matters get very complicated.

29

The gap in understanding is worse still when ideology becomes something sacred. I'm afraid of sacred issues, I try to stay focussed on the human level.

"The population segment most drenched in ideology is the Israeli settlers in the occupied territories. They have taken out of our holy writings a number of convictions which they hold to be above discussion, notably that every inch of Eretz-Israel is sacrosanct. It constitutes part of the Jewish heritage and must, they say, be restored to Israeli sovereignty, never mind who dwells there at the moment.

"This idea has to be refuted, and it's not easy. If anyone queries the dogmas of Gush Emunim, the visionary organization to which the settlers belong, they jump out of their skins. They live apart in a kind of spiritual seclusion. Nobody dares invade their privacy or call their beliefs into question. Their doctrine is thus self-perpetuating. They are infused with self-righteousness, believe in their own mission and, exposed as they are to a very real threat from the Arabs surrounding them, have developed a sense of martyrdom.

"I don't like it when minds are closed to

argument. What they are doing is so dangerous to our future, I must somehow reach their ears."

"If they will listen."

"They listen alright. They react angrily, emotionally, which suggests that in their heart of hearts they know there is another side to the argument.

"The problem, I tell them, must be considered seriously. We have here in Gaza, I point out, a diminutive stretch of land. It is one of the most densely populated areas of the world, one of the poorest, without water, without natural resources. Why should we take away, never mind a thousand dunams or a hundred dunams—even a single dunam? Why deprive them of the little land they have? We don't have to settle there; let them have the use of it. They are a people without a country, without a passport, without an official identity of any kind.

"However events turn out they are always the last in line, because they don't have the basic documents that every other person in the world possesses. Nobody will protect them. They were rejected by the Egyptians, they cannot be integrated into Israel—so what do we have in mind for them? We can't pretend they don't exist. By the turn of the century there will be a million dwellers in the Gaza Strip. If they don't ask, we must ask: what is their future, and what is ours?

"We provided them with full employment and that helped, yet they stay poor because they are so numerous. One of the problems with poverty is that people are immobile, unquestioning. Poverty is a passive acceptance of terrible conditions. Poverty is not just a financial predicament; it is a state of mind, a lack of stature. The poor are not just people who don't have money. They are people who don't have dignity, who don't have any answer to their dilemma, who don't have a chance to escape. What outcome is there, where is the hope?

"Problems stay unsolved for lack of budgets. Gaza is an occupied territory pending a peace settlement, therefore its inhabitants are administered by the military. They do not have the political authority to run their own affairs. Everything they try to do is subject to approval from above, from the military government. They feel intensely frustrated. Then comes the uprising."

\*        \*        \*

There is also the other, the hidden price....
I spent afternoons with professors, researchers, students from the five top scientific institutions. Israel's future in science and education was supposed to be the subject of our discussions.

The country's high-tech industries depend on its universities, which produce the engineers and scientists, not to mention the bulk of the basic research. Increasingly they are starved of money because the needs of defence come first. I heard complaints and complaints.

They are under-equipped although their work is crucial. In all countries funds are limited, this is a fact of life. It follows that the more is spent on arms, the less gets left for development. Israel's military budgets starve higher education of resources. What kind of national defence is that?

A dean from one of the universities told me: "We possess a computer-science department. The state of its equipment has to be seen to be believed. We have a hundred students, graduate students in computer science. We have twenty professors—and researchers, but just four personal computers."

He adds: "We expect our best students,

cc-c

33

those wanting to go all the way through their Ph.D. studies—and we know how many long years that takes—to make do with a grant of $400 a month. They start studying at a much later age than in America, because they have to do three years of military service before proceeding with their studies. They are older, many are married, they must have somewhere to live, and they study day and night with just enough to eat. They have to be saints or heroes, how long can it last?"

What goes on in these universities looks like a dismemberment of the army of knowledge.

I have to challenge Shimon Peres again:

"Israel has great potential, it should be able to master the knowledge revolution. Yet as things stand, according to what I hear from your professors and scientists, the job is not being done. When and how is the country going to change direction?"

He is aware of the shortcoming and it worries him more than he is ready to admit. He responds after a pause:

"During the last decade, it is true, education has suffered." He is talking of the period since the right-wing Likud came to power in 1977. "I would say that for the first seven years the government underestimated the importance of the universities. In the last three years" (since the Labour–Likud coalition took over) "there was another reason for delay: we had to cut all expenses dramatically in order to achieve economic recovery.

"After the elections this year we shall have to change our national priorities. But I look for ways and means even before that. Here is an example. I am trying to convince the Jewish Agency to concentrate on higher education in this country. At the moment it disperses its efforts in a variety of fields (agriculture, community development—all admittedly connected with its job, which is settling immigrants). I recommend that it devote itself to higher education and research.

"I imagine that the people at the universities have also told you that their work is not sufficiently appreciated. This is a repeated complaint, and I believe they are right. If we cannot pay high salaries to scientists, let us at least give them attention, recognize the importance of their work, create a climate that will keep up the morale of the scientific community. This would contribute to overcoming the malaise you have described."

The challenge of the "knowledge era" in Israel has been for a long period the substance

of my exchanges with Shimon Peres. Alone
among the country's leaders he devotes considerable thought to what new form the future
must take, for Israel and the whole region.

I said: "Peace and development are inter-
dependent, you are the first to point that out.
Without peace the country cannot forge
ahead. You have described to me how you
people can develop the Negev, how you can
develop all Israel, how you can help to
develop the whole region.

"Should Israel succeed in this mission it
may go further and contribute on the international scene to narrowing the yawning gap
between the industrial powers on the one
hand and the developing territories on the
other; to both of which groups, as it happens,
Israel belongs.

"All this is within your grasp—on one
condition, that you reduce your heavy military commitments. The peace process is
necessary for that; only then can you release
resources for other, more constructive
purposes. Israel's young pioneers will willingly mobilize their efforts. They already feel
that this is their real fight, this is their future.
Far indeed from the street battles, the violence
of today."

*"The world has become Jewish"*

Peres nods his agreement, adding that a nation's power is not measured exclusively by the size of its army. He goes further, seeking new horizons: "Israel used to be called a country of 'ein breira' or 'no alternative', because when you are in danger and under permanent threat of attack, you don't have a choice. You have to invest all your energy and resources in one thing—self-defence. The time has now come, with the use of logic and imagination, to create an alternative to the military posture.

"It must not be just an Israeli alternative but an alternative for our former enemies as well. People become very tense when they think they only have one road to travel. I wonder how long the two super-powers who have helped to maintain a high state of armament— the Russians by supplying weapons to countries that are aggressive, the Americans by providing help to Israel—can go on. The great thing about 'glasnost' is the right in Russia to pose questions. Traditionally the Russians have never liked questions. They liked dangers, they liked threats, they liked answers, but they never posed penetrating questions to themselves.

"The Russians are now beginning for the

first time to question themselves; and among the questions they will have to pose is what benefits do they get out of their huge investment in building up the armies of belligerent countries?

"Does it help those countries? Does it help the Soviet Union? Does it bear any fruit at all? One can ask all Russia's beneficiaries, from Cuba to Afghanistan, from Angola to Ethiopia: did Soviet aid improve your fate? Is the United States a weaker United States? Is the Soviet Union a stronger Soviet Union?

"All of us have to look for an alternative. Shall we continue to make our people suffer by investing again and again in armies which cannot provide long-term solutions? Or do we turn the other way and see how we can create new wealth and new opportunities?

"Questions cannot be suppressed any more, and they need answers. The spirit of enquiry is aroused, 'glasnost' is spreading. Information is moving like air. It is like a wind. A society can close the door; yet the slightest hole in the room can bring the wind in."

"Not only your country lags, Shimon Peres, the whole world is still largely unconscious of the new opportunities. The

European Economic Community allocates 70 per cent of its collective budget for price support in agriculture, and almost nothing for the new technologies. All that money gone to waste subsidizing products the Europeans cannot sell. Instead of developing knowledge, as my friends at the Israeli universities would like to do, they go on investing in the past.

"Here we see that not only the two superpowers are stuck in a rut, obsessed and undermined as they are by their military vendettas, but a whole civilized continent with no conquests in mind has failed so far to focus on the big challenge of our day: creating and mastering the new tools of knowledge.

"Israel's choice should be to take up the modern challenge and show by example what is the right way to use the energy, the brains and the resources of a people."

"I hope that will happen," says Peres. "Israel does not have the tradition and the past of Europe. Life results not only from the laws we make in our own times but from the precedents created by previous generations. We miss those precedents because our history started just forty years ago."

"As a nation, but not as a people."

"As a people in its own land. Before we

39

were dispersed all over the globe, speaking different tongues, poised in different national attitudes, indoctrinated with different views and habituated to different traditions. Our reunification here is a curious culture-mix. It is a confluence of separate waters in order to create a single stream that will flow more steadily and fruitfully."

"You told me that a Japanese industrialist who visited you the other day said: 'The world would be helped by a partnership between Japan and Israel.' What does he mean?"

"I have thought about it. As a distant ambition it is something to be taken seriously, Israel and Japan could become friends and allies.

"An interesting book appeared called 'The Japanese and the Jews', written by a Japanese author. He compares the history of our two peoples. He says the Japanese were traditionally worried about earthquakes, fire, old age and strangers. The Jews were worried about invaders, big and threatening empires, dryness, lack of water and the small size of the nation. We see that each has developed its own characteristics in accordance with its own history.

## *"The world has become Jewish"*

"The Jews had no motherland. The Japanese had little land in their overcrowded islands, and scarce resources. Both have had to make a supreme effort to overcome their difficulties. That supreme effort has, yes, in similar ways, sharpened their minds and given them the energy to cope with every circumstance. It is this extra, the need to do something extra, that has vested them with a measure of extra talent. The "extra" became second nature.

"So here we see, now we come to think of it, a strange meeting between two peoples isolated either by nature or by fate, sharpening their talents and their senses so as to exist. This might lead, as you suggest, to a common venture in the future."

"There may be more," I added. "If anything can be compared to the Holocaust which decimated the Jewish people, it is the atomic explosion that struck the Japanese. Apart from the physical damage caused, it had a profound impact on the national psyche. The Japanese are the only people to have faced the nuclear fire in full force, with tens of thousands killed on the spot and hundreds of thousands condemned to a later death, all these fates sealed in one instant. The soul of the Japanese was for a time shattered. They had to reconstruct it, as the Jewish people had to reconstruct theirs after the Holocaust. The two countries have this in common as well."

"The two ordeals are not strictly comparable. Still, as a rabbi in the US said: 'A nuclear bomb is an airborne Auschwitz.' And the Jewish author Elie Wiesel: 'With the invention of nuclear weapons the world has become Jewish.' Namely it has started to worry about its very existence and survival—an anxiety that was formerly monopolized by the Jews."

"All the same, is it not unreal to think of linking two countries so far apart, Israel and Japan?"

"The world is changing at such a speed that our imagination lags behind. Things happen differently nowadays and we must keep our minds open to see surprising combinations and novel roles, which would not have appeared logical years and even months ago."

Yesterday in my Jerusalem room I received a call (in French) from Bir-Zeit, the university so close to one of the hearts of the uprising—the city of Ramallah on the road leading north from Jerusalem. The caller wanted to tell me that he and his university colleagues,

Palestinian militants, had discussed the conclusion of my book *The World Challenge*, proposing a common development of the West and the Third World in coordination, through the new computer sciences.

Amid the uproar of hate this was a signal. Can we now start to build the reconciliation of peoples towards an era of cooperation in this region? How far is Shimon Peres prepared to go?

He is first and foremost a pioneer of the Jewish state. Like Ben-Gurion he devoted all his life to organizing its defence, to striving for the maintenance of a military superiority. Can this background of thought and experience allow a leap into the future, carrying the younger generation with him to new horizons so different from the forty years of endless wars that forged his own generation? Is he satisfied it can be done? Does he devote enough thought to overcome the prejudices and other obstacles which stand in the way?

He understands that men's ideas are changing as they never did before. "Human history," he observes, "is a history of mutations, but never did they occur at such a speed. What used to take a thousand years may now take a thousand days or less. It is an unbelievable pace. So we must watch not only the changes but the speed at which they occur. We must endeavour to understand them, so as to be if possible ahead of the storm and not at the end of it."

"If Israel succeeds in becoming a land of knowledge, will this help the region? The Arabs are not particularly well disposed towards Israel, they may prefer to seek guidance from others countries."

"The Arab world," answers Peres broodingly, "keeps asking itself: what went wrong with our history? For generations we were among the forerunners in human development, in science, in arts, in astronomy, in constructing the largest buildings, in putting up the lofty pyramids, in creating a lucid grammar before anybody else, in tackling mathematics, chemistry and other important subjects. What happened, where did we lose this sense of progress? I believe the Arab world is in search of an answer to this very painful question.

"Israel may help; it has managed to adapt the scientific potential around it to national development. Spurred by this example, the Arabs could rediscover their old momentum. We have one advantage over the super-powers, and that is our smallness. We cannot really endanger anybody. We are too small to be dangerous, while the United States and the Soviet Union are too large to be comforting. Nobody who looks at our history can suspect us of becoming an empire. We cannot: we don't have the size, or the land, or the people, or the inclination to become a big power.

"Traditionally we were small in history, small in numbers, small in land. The only escape we have from the limit of size is in the spiritual domain, but never in physical dimensions. So we cannot endanger any other country. It also goes against our history to dominate another people. The aim in Jewish philosophy is to dominate ourselves, quite a difficult job. Whoever tries to subjugate somebody else is endangering himself. All the empires that ruled over us have disappeared."

"I'm not sure," I said, "that everybody would consider your country so inoffensive today. You say Israel cannot frighten anyone because it is not an empire. But remember the famous indictment by De Gaulle when suddenly he became enraged against Israel in 1967 and blasted 'Jewish power', saying: 'The Jews are a people over-confident and bent on domination.' He was a man of chosen words.

The Chosen and the Choice

He accused Israel of being an imperialist-minded society, rising to dominate others. And he was not alone as you know. This goes with what many people think, including of course the Arabs."

"My answer is that De Gaulle was wrong in his description of the Jewish people. History shows it. May I make a personal remark? I had the chance of meeting De Gaulle and was struck by his brilliance and control of words. Yet I was surprised how little he knew about the Jewish people. Even when he describes the Nazi danger in his book of memoirs, he shows little understanding for the Jewish tragedy. He said the Six Day War would start a third world conflict. Well, it did not. After all if we are really so dominating, why did we give Sinai back to Egypt—though it is double the size of the whole state of Israel—and that without shooting a single cartridge? We did it twice, once after the 1956 war and again after the 1973 war. No, if the Israelis wanted to become a dominating people, they would betray their Jewish heritage."

"Then why do you keep military control over the Palestinians?"

"On the face of it, we are entitled to control of this land. That is admittedly not very gratifying to the Arabs resident in Palestine. Their feelings must be taken into account, because we are aiming for peace."

"There is an answer, I suggest: to share territories between the two populations."

Shimon Peres explains the difficulties as he sees them:

"The country is small and cannot easily be split. It is precisely because Palestine is so diminutive that the aspiration of the Jews to recover this particular land can scarcely be viewed as territorial imperialism. Compare its size per Jewish inhabitant with the size of other countries. Only a handful suffer such a great population density. And that is without counting the Arabs, who increase the population further.

"All Israeli Jews believe—to quote the Balfour Declaration—that Palestine is the national home of the Jewish people; but only a part of them want to keep it all. This maximalist group divides into two sub-groups which overlap each other: those who believe that Eretz-Israel belongs to the Jewish people for historic and religious reasons; and those who fear that withdrawal from the West Bank and Gaza would make the remainder indefensible.

"The realistic part of the Jewish community believe that ruling over 1.5m. foreigners against their will inflates defence costs, calling into question the utility even in strategic terms of holding on to these densely populated territories."

"What restrains you from putting this group's readiness for withdrawal into effect?"

"If Palestine is small, Israel is smaller still and even less defensible. Therefore a treaty is needed fixing recognized frontiers and ensuring that peace is kept. Unfortunately partners to negotiation on the Arab side have not been forthcoming—so far. Perhaps we have been too nervous about how to get the talks started."

Meanwhile the Israelis control the Palestinians, a minority in their land. They have done so for twenty years; and the result is hard to distinguish from colonialism.

\*　　\*　　\*

Peres said once: the Jewish people loses its raison d'être if it imposes rule by force. I have no doubt about his sincerity. But does he fully realize the meaning of the uprising in what are called the occupied territories?

After twenty years of Israeli occupation, the Palestinians have taken their fate in their hands. By their spontaneous, and repeated riots the new generation has turned itself into a nation.

Israel's soldiers who try to repress this upheaval formed yesterday a young and highly motivated army. One against ten they faced the Arab world. Today they have become guardians of law and order, they do the work of policemen. Their malaise is so extreme—thankfully—that army head-quarters announced recently, to reassure the parents, that trained psychiatrists were being sent to monitor any emotional disturbances.

While these events are happening Shimon Peres finds time to continue our regular sessions about long-term issues, notably the remarkable scientific breakthroughs that are within reach in this country. We see how the whole region could be irrigated with new waters to wash away old hostilities and make possible the emergence of more hopeful prospects. Is it all a dream?

\*　　　\*　　　\*

CC-D

"Here we need to retain our political logic," concludes Peres. "We must be very careful not to give the impression that in suggesting a joint scientific and economic effort in the Middle East, we are cunningly evading the need to hammer out a settlement of our conflict with the Arabs. We shouldn't create the feeling that knowledge or economics is pushed forward as a replacement for the negotiation of a political solution. That is not the case."

"What are you implying?"

"Instead of dealing with issues of territory and issues of sovereignty, we could declare: we shall bring you knowledge, we shall share it with you. I say, no, that is not how to start. Let us deal with the question of who will govern whom, who will govern what, separately from these more general matters; so that the new opportunities for knowledge are not a replacement but an additive.

"There is an inherent suspicion among the Arabs that we hunt around for subjects to talk about and that we want to escape the major issue, the major conflict. We should explain carefully: look, we are ready to sit down with you and deal with the sources of the conflict 'per se'. We should add that once we solve the

## "The world has become Jewish"

conflict new horizons will open before us with possibilities, if we wish it, of doing things together, in cooperation."

## 3

# The leadership question

I cross the famous Allenby bridge, kept open uninterruptedly since the Six Day War. Though not much as bridges go, it has provided a steady contact between two worlds. Only a few miles from Jericho and less than half-an-hour from Jerusalem, it is crossed daily by people on their way to Jordan and the Arab Middle East.

Two-thirds of the population in the Hashemite kingdom are Palestinians, brethren to those living across the river under Israeli occupation. For the Israelis, the ideal would be to have Jordan take all the West Bank Palestinians under its care, which would mean negotiation for control of that zone by King Hussein. Let him keep order there, relieving the Israeli army of distracting responsibilities.

But that has happened—unsuccessfully—before. The Jordanians ruled the West Bank for almost twenty years till 1967; and the

Palestinians have not forgotten that experience. Every conversation (with those over 20) leads back to the massacre of Black September and what they describe as the "nightmare of Jordanian domination". Militants in the occupied territories would take the same kind of action against the re-imposition of Jordanian rule as they do against the Israeli occupation today. They have won the day, because in August King Hussein publicly refused to represent them.

Back with Shimon Peres at his home in the evening. His wish would be nevertheless to settle the Palestine problem directly with Amman. Perhaps a federative relation between the two banks of the Jordan might allay Palestinian anxieties.

Our conversation becomes more general. We recognize that history imposes its own shackles. Conservatism in external affairs derives from traditionalism in local affairs. "Let us have a look at the domestic scene," says Peres. "I think two or three obstacles prevent an economic take-off in Arab countries.

"They remain, as they themselves confess, excessively oriented towards agriculture. They don't have industry because they are not open to industry. Many are accustomed still to count their wealth and potential in accordance with the number of dunams they cultivate, or even the number of dunams they own. Only now are they beginning to understand that the problem is not how many dunams you have but what the yield is per dunam.

"When we argue with Arab inhabitants on this side of the Jordan, they say: you took away our land. We say: we took away only a part of your land, and that for purposes essential to your welfare as well as ours—to build an infra-structure, to supply electricity, telephones, to develop the area. That should not hold up progress, there is plenty of land left if it is used properly. On the same number of dunams it is possible to produce eight times, nine times more than in the past. We do it, and there is no reason why you should not do the same, the resources are at your disposal.

"So the problem is very specific, you see? In a modern society, agriculture may be an occupation for a mere 2 per cent of the population, with the rest engaged in science, industry, information, services. That is a historic transformation, difficult to stomach. The Arabs are proud first and foremost of their land. As one of them told me: 'Take my wife, don't take my land.'

"There is another problem, and they are aware of it: the structure of their society. It is based on the extended family or tribe. In an Arab village, relatives live side by side. Comes a new generation, and they may add a floor to the parental home. Inside the place is clean and neat, but they will not invest an inch of effort outside the house. They will not invest in roads, in sewage, in services, medical or other, in the development of their villages. They realize, I think, that they have to grow out of this totally rural concept, that they have to escape from their houses.

"Here then are the two faces of the existing situation. The Arabs are today divided between the sector that clings to the past and the sector that looks to the future.

"Those who reject or are disillusioned with modern life follow in the wake of the Ayatollah Khumeini, who calls for purity, restraint, sacrifice and compensation in paradise. That is what 'fundamentalism' is about, an escape from the real challenges of our changing times.

"Arabs in the other sector try to understand how to elevate their society, how to place it on the moving-belt in the modern world."

## The leadership question

Shimon Peres speaks easily of the Arabs, he knows a lot about their history and literature. Yet the word Palestinian seems to cause him a momentary qualm, associated perhaps with the many killings of the PLO. His intelligence quickly regains control, though a visible hesitation is felt each time.

From the few stalled seconds in our otherwise open and articulate exchanges, I conjecture what this indicates for the bulk of the Israeli people. Behind Shimon Peres's reflex I perceive the barrier between the two societies, following on a century of bickering, animosity, and worse. It would be crazy to underestimate the magnitude of the holdup. My conversations with Peres, so candid on many subjects, are most revealing on this point. He does not attempt to conceal the moment of struggle between his instincts and his intelligence. At such times the intricacy of the problem strikes me forcibly and arouses my doubts. Can the creativity of the future overcome the prejudices and conflicts of the past?

*    *    *

A memory relating to one of my first intrusions into politics comes to mind. Forty years ago I was a very young journalist on *Le Monde*, whose editor invited me to write leading articles and to select my own subjects for investigation in the area of foreign affairs. My first trip in 1948 was to the French occupation-zone of Germany. I returned quite disturbed. Were we going to leave the Germans vanquished, disarmed and humiliated? Should we not seize this unique opportunity to forge an historic association?

Back from Germany I applied through my editor for an audience with the first post-war French president, the socialist Vincent Auriol. I explained to him what I saw as the opportunity of the moment. Let us offer the Germans, I said, an equal partnership in a European union with France. I still remember every word of the reply given by that albeit wise and responsible statesman: "I like your generous ideas, my young friend, but you are in too great a hurry. Nothing of this kind can be accomplished so soon after the great tragedy of war. Wound-healing takes time. In twenty years or so you will probably be right and your generation will be able to approach the task. Today no-one would understand, and we can only spoil the chances for the future. Be patient."

A few weeks later I met Jean Monnet. He

was a statesman of a different kind, eager for rational change. Though merely a planning commissioner at the time, he was more impatient even than me to launch the work of Franco-German coexistence. He gave me a meticulous dissertation. I recall him sitting at a low table. Behind him on the wall hung a map of Europe with a hard-drawn circle surrounding France and Germany.

A few weeks later he would found the Coal–Steel Pool, which later became the Common Market, opening the road to Europe. His vision and not the old wisdom proved to be right.

The Palestinians present a similar dilemma. Will Shimon Peres in the coming months adopt the cautious wisdom of Vincent Auriol, or will he opt for the daring spirit of Jean Monnet? The fate of this dispute, a focal issue in the present world, will be not less decisive for the future of the Middle East than the Franco-German alliance was for the future of Europe; perhaps more so.

I say to Peres: "Everyone knows the Arabs are divided. The question I now ask refers to the Israelis. Are they not just as deeply divided in their own way between left and right, between religious and secular? Do they all share the same interpretation of their past, do they all envisage the same future?

"I do not see true unity among Israelis on such important matters as holding the territories, or making up the intellectual and cultural tissue of the future. I feel the presence of two ideologies in Israel; and this conflict lives intensely inside you. Out of your country's unrelenting domestic struggle could some rapprochement emerge with one or other part of the Arab world in this region?"

Peres does not, I feel, want his people to be divided, possibly because he is himself divided. He struggles to reconcile the two parts of his own being, as he tries to heal the breach in society. Thus he tends to externalize the conflict.

Israelis do not acknowledge the extent to which the war has shifted from their borders and is now fought in the heart of the country. The battle is no longer located on the Golan, on the Jordan, in Sinai; it is waged inside Israel's cities. Combat rages within the walls, and this is what Peres must deal with. Needed today is less the courage of a Winston Churchill in mobilizing forces against the foreign aggressor, than the resolution of an Abraham Lincoln in overcoming civil strife.

## The leadership question

Peres: "In Israel the problem is not the divisions, they are natural, but how we deal with them. All Israelis have equal rights; whatever views they have can be freely expressed. The ones whose interests lie in science or industry can go ahead, can even run ahead. On more controversial subjects we seek a mandate at the polling-booth."

He accepts the democratic process. Laudably he goes with the tide; but is that enough? My doubts find expression: "I would like to share your faith in democracy. In normal times I agree that the system works. On the other hand when the hour of crisis comes, democracy doesn't usually seem to provide exceptional leadership. This has been the tragedy of Europe in the present century. It explains a recent decline in America, is it not a problem in Israel today?"

Such ideas do not appeal to him, and his feelings are strong on the matter. "Israel has been independent for forty years," he declares, "and they have been forty years of crisis. Not many countries have undergone five wars in so short a spell. We showed that a democratic country can overcome these ordeals without losing battles and without losing freedom either. I think about

61

it quite often.

"Never did a situation of emergency, even a war emergency, induce us to restrict freedom. Look at present happenings, you see a fierce debate in Israel over issues of life and death. Is the freedom of press, the freedom of television impaired in any way?

"Israel has shown wisdom and restraint as a democracy even, on many occasions—let us be frank—without great leadership. The phrase 'great leadership' needs to be redefined: is it in truth a healthy recipe? When you look at history, why were there so many destructive wars? Because of the so-called great leaders, inciting or exacerbating war. Good leaders in normal life do not need to be heroes. Read Tolstoy again on Napoleon. In history when you kill a lot of people you are instantly great. When you try to save lives you are small. I prefer the smallness of saving life to the greatness of killing people."

\*          \*          \*

Shimon Peres faces a dilemma about leadership. His basic conviction is democratic. There is no ambiguity about that: he fully accepts the common will and majority rule. But bold authority may be needed if the

people of Israel are to be prised away from the
habit of endless war; that is my view at any
rate. Might not the critical leap toward peace
necessitate draconian leadership?

"Throughout most of his life," I remarked,
"a statesman is powered by a normal measure
of personal ambition. There comes a point
when an emergency reaches crisis propor-
tions, calling on all the philosophy, wisdom
and experience he has accumulated. At that
moment personal ambition ceases to be a
dominant motive.

"Instead a sense of mission takes over, and
the leader becomes selfless. Israel is not at war
at this moment officially, but it is so 'de facto'.
You know it and see it. The crisis is here, with
violence every day, with the future unclear,
with the need for tough, delicate, profound
decisions. All of this cries out for leadership."

Peres: "You are right, with one qualifica-
tion: the leader must stay in tune with the will
of the people. This is an overriding principle.
We are talking about democracy. I would say
that democracy is more than just a system, it is
a vision. It is not only a body, it is also a soul.

"The same applies to leadership. Yes, you
need a sense of mission, you should have
courage, you need determination, you have to

be patient, you must never be afraid. But you know, not all problems can be solved by a nod of the head. There are many uncertainties. On what issue for example do you take a stand?

"It can be a matter of timing. You win a war a minute after you thought you had lost it. Those that can last out an extra minute or an extra day may win the battle; and the same goes for a political battle. Probably you find me too dilatory in the political field, but who knows?

"I would say that the sense of mission is more important than the urge to leadership; and maybe the pursuit of a mission is what makes leadership an important instrument in a democratic society."

"But you said the other day that we should speak about the heavy price which will have to be paid if the process of peace is not seriously pursued, or if peace is not tried, or if it fails."

"Let us go from the obvious to the less obvious," answers Shimon Peres. The obvious is that we would endanger Israel's survival if we did not remain a Jewish state, that is, a state with a majority of Jews. In a democracy you don't weigh the people, you count them. Democracy is in practice arithmetical—it deals with quantity, not quality.

An Arab state is a state where the Arabs are the majority. If we lose our numerical preponderance our state stops being Jewish. That is the first point.

"Again the obvious: if we do not progress, we shall regress. We shall find ourselves deteriorating again to the stage of belligerency, and much of what was achieved in preparing for peace will disappear. Relations with Egypt can become tense again. Whoever calls for war may then have a more receptive audience in the Arab world.

"The deterioration begins with threats; then it becomes an arms race; after that you live in a climate of suspicion, and before you know it everything you initiate becomes self-propelled. If you go in the direction of war it is self-propulsion. If you make for peace you are lucky, because self-propulsion works here too.

"The third danger—and this is something Israel must be careful about—is that instead of escaping from world isolation we may find ourselves isolated more than ever before. Even when governments voted against us in the United Nations, public opinion abroad was on our side; and that is a very important strength.

CC-E

"Today if we do not take the initiative for peace we shall find that we lose out in the public opinion stakes, which worries me a lot. Israel always enjoyed tremendous popular support in France, in England, in the United States, even in countries like Yugoslavia—even in the Soviet Union.

"But if we lose the backing of public opinion, then for the first time we may see a combination of hostility on the diplomatic front and disapproval on the part of ordinary people. It may be happening right now."

I decided to put the issue before him squarely: "Every people has a quite normal tendency to be nationalist or patriotic. Right wingers in this country equate patriotism with a Greater Israel—with holding as much territory as possible. This is the message from the right. Now you, as I read your speeches, express a different kind of patriotism. You say, we want a truly Jewish state, a state with a philosophy, a state with a message.

"The present debate in this country reveals two kinds of patriotism. *Patriotism of territory, and patriotism of identity.* Which will represent the soul of this nation?"

# 4

# Explosion of a generation

Last night in Jerusalem I strolled along the silent streets, desolate under a curfew imposed by the Israelis—the first since they had reunited the capital in 1967. To live in Jerusalem is to be caressed by the wings of history. Legendary past events have, each and every one of them, left their visible mark.

I viewed the ancient fortifications, the El Aksa mosque, the Dome of the Rock, and further along on Mount Zion the Chamber of Martyrs, the tomb of King David in the shadow of the Mount of Olives. Jerusalem has been destroyed many times, yet lives still and thrives as well as it ever did before. I have a feeling that its current discords will eventually be resolved. We must believe this, and here it can be believed.

The need is to rise above preconceived ideas. There is a higher collective interest transcending all separate interests. Jean Monnet understood that European union could not be achieved unless the participating nations rose above their old-fashioned parochialism.

"Experience has shown," he writes, "that those who believe they understand me are no better than others at drawing the consequences. The act of negotiation is so natural to them that they see it as an end in itself. We are here, I say, not to negotiate for each party's separate advantage, but to seek in common the collective advantage. Only in this manner shall we be able to eliminate particularist approaches."

Monnet's fresh and fecund vision gave birth to Europe. He died, buried under an embarrassed silence in Gaullist France, ignored by the general himself who saw in him a person without nationality, a foreign agent, the embodiment of anti-France. But years later in early 1988, the Elysee of François Mitterrand transferred the ashes of Jean Monnet to the Pantheon, with widespread approval. The first creator of peace resting among the warriors of our history. A new era indeed.

The Arab–Israeli struggle will not escape the influence of his inspiring mind. He sensed that an arrangement had to be devised which would give each side the feeling of belonging to a greater whole. This can only be achieved if all sides pursue single-mindedly the "common advantage".

Again I meet with Shimon Peres. I am aware of his difficulties. He is subject to the inane ban on deals with the immediate adversary, the PLO, with whom he must have nothing to do. Will he throw off this shackle?

Sonia, Peres's caring and unobtrusive wife, who never speaks publicly, prepares as always a quiet evening for us. Here in Jerusalem whenever the violence of the Palestinian upheaval leaves time to look beyond present events, I am gripped by the opportunity offered by this new and bloody chapter of Jewish history.

Today is the fiftieth anniversary of Crystal Night (Kristallnacht), when under the pretext of a Jewish plot the entire Nazi Germany launched, on Hitler's personal orders, a "Jew hunt"; prelude to the Final Solution, the Holocaust.

"You know," I remind Peres, "this terrible occasion is commemorated everywhere today. It was a decisive moment, wasn't it? The outbreak of violence and hate by the Nazis—which paradoxically sparked the march of the Jewish people towards its true destiny. Israel's independence came into being on that night. And that night began Hitler's historic march towards his own perdition."

Peres relaxes. He has abandoned his former reluctance to mention Hitler. The racist passions, converted by the Führer into a totalitarian regime of conquest, still live in his memory; if only because their aftermath is still to be found in many places, stirring hot embers beneath the ashes.

"This sombre anniversary," Peres reflects, "revives several questions from the past. One is the question of Hitler himself. There are rare examples in history where a man like Hitler actually foresaw all the mistakes—and then proceeded to make them.

"He was outspoken about the perils of fighting on two fronts; upon which he made war on two fronts. He derisively criticized the fatal adventure of Napoleon into Russia. He went and repeated it.

"After that, as you recalled the other day, he did what best served Stalin's purpose. Having invaded Russia's land and people, he undertook a scorched earth policy. He made his soldiers denude the territory, without understanding that they themselves would die from winter and hunger on the endless stretches that they had devastated."

"Hitler's state," I inserted, "also exiled Einstein, the scientific genius of the century, to the United States, where his theories allowed the Americans to develop the atomic bomb."

Peres concluded that there was basically a madness in Hitler. "But," he went on, "a madness is also a system. It derives its strength from the fact that people are not over-attached to known civilized standards. Hitler had a very sharp mind. Madmen are not affected by norms or conventions, nor are they taken in by existing beliefs and prejudices. In a way a madman is a free man. He is free from moral inhibitions, like a wild animal in the jungle.

"From the Jewish point of view another thesis was killed in the gas chambers; the thesis of assimilation. It had not made headway from the beginning. When the Age of Reason came in the 18th Century the Jews felt liberated from their spiritual segregation. They opened their minds to Western culture in a movement called the Enlightenment.

"They were full of hope in this new world. They thought something basic had changed. So long as spiritual darkness prevailed in medieval times the Jews had not been surprised by the kind of life they were forced to endure.

*The Chosen and the Choice*

"Christianity at the beginning had some cruel expressions, as you know: the abuses of the Roman Empire, the Spanish Inquisition. The Jews retired to their ghettoes and were separated from the rest of the world. They lived austerely, deprived of the luxuries and earthly achievements available to the gentile world. All that at the time had little bearing on Jewish life, based as it was exclusively on the Talmud. I make an exception of the short intermezzo when Jews were part of Spanish culture, before their expulsion in 1492.

"At long last the world began to alter. There was talk of liberty, equality, fraternity. The Jewish people were dazzled at first, until they discovered that the universal brotherhood was not for them. New prejudices arose to replace the old religious ones. During the 19th Century nationalism acquired racialist overtones.

"Yet cultural assimilation was strong. In Germany men tried to be loyal patriots while continuing to believe in the faith of Moses. Many good Jews thought they could merge into the Teutonic fatherland by cutting themselves off from the Jewish people in the social sense, confining their Judaism to the synagogue.

*Explosion of a generation*

"Judaism is at once a nationalism and a religion. They decided to become German nationalists and Jewish religionists. The contribution of the Jewish people to German culture was immense in all domains. They were impressed by their own participation, and were seduced by the German Weltanschauung they had adopted.

"What we then saw is that cruelty is stronger than creativity. Cruel individuals can run their mad race with tremendous speed, outpacing the more kindly people who try to retain educated values. The attempt at assimilation failed.

"The price that the Jewish people paid is enormous. Today in 1988 there are in absolute terms less Jews in the world than existed at the beginning of the century. In 1900 they numbered 17m., today the figure is only 13m.

"The Jews have traditionally paid with their lives for the survival of their beliefs and for their continued existence as a nation. Hitler wiped out one-third of the world's Jewish population, but revitalized the survivors into becoming at last a united Jewish community. Their affliction brought them a sense of solidarity, a sense of purpose, and it made Israel.

"Well before Hitler, Jews in Eastern Europe began to recognize that living passively on the fringes of a foreign culture was not the answer. They had to revive their own culture, which meant going back to original sources.

"So even before we started to return to our motherland, we returned to our ancient mother-tongue. There was a renewal of the Hebrew language which until then had only been a language for prayers. In Poland and Russia, Jewish schools were opened where Hebrew was used not only for prayer but for education. I myself for example, born in White Russia, was taught in Hebrew at a school in a chain called 'Tarbut' or culture.

"This moment was the beginning of our final awakening. It did not go easily. There were in those days many schools of thought among the Jews. Some opposed the Zionists' proposed concentration of the Jewish people in Palestine. But with Hitler's tragedy came a realization of our historic past and a mobilization. Mobilization for life, mobilization for existence, mobilization to carry on our role in history.

"While the Bible enabled us to exist as a people without a land, our dispersal as an eternal minority exposed us to cruelty, to hatred, to perpetual victimization. Moses Hess said: 'Even if they accept our gospel, they don't like our noses.' The Nazis brought things to a head, they exploded our last illusions. This time we had to discover our historical response, find our land, create our state."

*      *      *

I read a letter from Shimon Peres to the president of the World Union of Jewish Students on the anniversary of Crystal Night. He wrote that the first lesson to be learnt was the need for a Jewish state. "The second major lesson," he continued, "was the imperative obligation, on our own soil and wherever Jews live, never to accept any form of intolerance, persecution or racial discrimination."

That letter, sent from Jerusalem to Brussels, was dated December 1987. Only a few days later the "events", as they are called, started brutally throughout the occupied territories. They have not ceased at the time of writing.

Will the vital instinct of the young Palestinian rioters lead to the birth of the Palestinian nation? Proponents of that idea should avoid past mistakes and listen to the wisdom of Jean Monnet, who urged the cooperation of neighbouring countries in hammering out a common future.

I come across urgent calls from Jews in anguish for a revision of old doctrines. The head of a religious high school in Jerusalem writes: "On this our 40th anniversary I cannot help seeing our nation as beset with pain and anguish. We feel lost. I wonder what Isaiah would say today if he were among us, leaning against the walls of Jerusalem.

"There is nothing new under the sun, have we not always destroyed our achievements with our own hands? Can we not recall before our eyes a whole two-thousand-year history of recurrent self-destruction? I dream that some day I shall be able to tell my pupils about the rediscovery of the good life in our God-given land. We must do something more than just perpetuate our defence by military means. We have to heal the wounds in ourselves and our enemies, we have to re-invent peace. Yes, a more far-seeing form of Zionism."

Looking to Peres, I suggest: "Something new, it seems, must be created in the spiritual field by the Jewish people, if they want an Israel that is faithful to its destiny and able to fulfil its potential."

"That is so. After forty years we have to decide which way to turn. We have to make a choice.

"Yesterday in the Cabinet we had an interesting meeting. One of the ministers stood up and said: 'I remember as a child co-existing with the Arabs and I know we can co-exist. My father—and mother—understood them. All we have to do is treat them equally.'

"I told him, look, you have a problem: you keep returning to your childhood and your memories. In the meantime there is a different Arab world. Our problem now, and I mean now, is not to remember the past but to imagine the future. A new generation has grown up. The Arabs have multiplied in number, and that too creates a new situation.

"Try to remember the Gaza Strip twenty years ago. It contained only 300,000 Arabs. Today their number exceeds 600,000, and the size of the Strip hasn't changed. Yet there is not a peep out of us about their future. So what help are your memories? Our problem is to think out what is going to be their future.

"When I speak about a new Zionism, I speak about a Zionism offering peace, making peace, structuring a peace that should be as meaningful to our neighbours as it is to ourselves.

"Others have a different version of the new Zionism. They talk of a return to religion in the narrow sense, religion as a cult, religion as an organization. But again I repeat that Judaism is first and foremost a moral commitment, it is not just the membership of a group. What kept us alive was our moral commitment, that is the essence.

"After forty years of war, belligerence and agony we have to see the Promised Land in a different light. We have won independence and we have gained strength. We have to give our nationhood a new meaning.

"Jews have never tried to convert others to the Jewish faith. As a people we have always carried a mission of our own, a mission of peace; and if we lose sight of this aim and purpose, we shall discover how defenceless we are. We must remember that the main source of strength is the spirit of a people. The job of our body is to defend the spirit, not to replace it."

# 5

# A new kind of hero

While in Jerusalem I read Gorbachev's speech (this was in February) repeating his fear that Reagan's insistence on the Stars Wars programme might revive the arms race.

He added: "If the military build-up, that we slowed down a little last year, starts this time in space, we shall be moving towards a profound destabilization. We shall have to stop the disarmament programme that was agreed upon. Responsible will be America's renewed drive for space weapons."

Not only will the détente be affected, the development of the United States' own economy is at stake. When I left the US to come and work in Jerusalem, the automatic annual reduction in the federal budget (a reduction designed to offset five previous years of boom in military expenses) had started to undermine drastically all support for research, laboratories, universities and fellowships.

One of the consequences for the students themselves was the increase in tuition fees at the top-graded universities to $13,000 a year and more. Fees are highest in the best scientific institutes (Stanford, MIT, Carnegie-Mellon etc.) where a constantly rising tide of foreign students apply for admission, financially supported by their own governments.

How much does the US spend on the military? Up to 7 per cent of its gross national product, which weighs heavily on other needs. And America's 7 per cent is itself much less than the 15 to 20 per cent estimated for Soviet military expenses. In Jerusalem the new budget for 1988 allocates 18 per cent to the military side. This compares with 6 per cent made available for all the Israeli government's civilian investments.

"As we can see," I point out to Peres, "the real enemy is not always the one we can denounce publicly. It can be this vicious crushing weight: preparations for war; which can be, as you observed yourself, the equivalent of actual war.

"The relative decline of US economic efficiency is potentially, I feel, the preface to tragedy.

"Not only America's financial base but also

its technological base is deteriorating. The space programme in the US has been troubled by a succession of accidents. The reason is not mechanical, there are much deeper considerations. The military-industrial complex deflects a disproportionate part of the nation's resources away from constructive purposes.

"America's creative power is being slowly eroded. The number of young students completing courses in the crucial scientific disciplines falls short of the need. Almost two-thirds of the candidates for a doctorate in these fields at American universities are foreigners, half of whom go back to their home countries after graduating.

"In the academic world America has been *and remains the cradle of the whole knowledge revolution.* Its research institutes are unchallenged in this new era. They are a magnet attracting the best minds: *the American university has turned into a world university.*

"But the country has failed to use this revolution for its own advantage. Other nations, notably in Asia, have been allowed to exploit America's theoretical discoveries, putting them to practical use. The industrial benefit has thus accrued far from America's shores,

cc-f

to the profit of territories with low military budgets but sound investment policies."

Shimon Peres is familiar with military budgets, having been in his time deputy minister and later minister of defence. "I really don't know enough about the United States," he says. "But I agree with you, one of the greatest problems is the continual increase in America's outgoings on weaponry.

"Military outlays however are not all wasted. I would classify the research and development done as the productive part of this expenditure, because it produces from time to time new methods, new materials, new combinations. Most modern techniques originated in work connected with the armed forces. As long as the military spends its money on research and development, that is not too bad.

"*The minute you begin to produce the actual hardware—in the absence of war—you start bleeding the economy.* Moreover military hardware has to be changed every seven years at a cost 3 or 4 times greater on each occasion. Our next plane will cost three times as much as the plane now in use. There is no economy that can increase its gross national product threefold or fourfold every seven years.

"So military expenditure goes up by elevator, while economic development can only use the staircase. The gap between the two is widening all the time.

"The sensible way to run a military establishment is: lavish outlays on research and development, prudent frugality when it comes to big-volume output. It is the production side that endangers the economy, not, I believe, the research side.

"I am aware of General Eisenhower's warning, when he left the presidency in 1960, about the great danger presented by the military-industrial complex. He was right, but the primacy of this complex was not laid down by Moses on Mount Sinai. It is fed by pressure, appetites, ambitions. And it can be controlled.

"What you and I are talking about is the need to replace an old vocation, the military, with a new one, scientific creativity: and to restructure budgetary priorities so as to justify the new emphasis. We face a serious change of course. All energies and all thinking methods should be focussed on this process of stepping from one era to the next. Here lies the true meaning, I feel, of our discussion and our quest."

# The Chosen and the Choice

*       *       *

The above anxieties and hopes are echoed by other authoritative voices, which do not seem intimidated any longer. The Rector of Haifa University, Professor Gavriel Ben-Dor, has just published a documented report which concludes with these words:

"The time has come to cut defence spending and concentrate on renewing economic growth, techno-scientific progress, education and welfare. This will make us stronger economically, and incidentally better able to handle another arms race should one be forced on us in the future."

The Rector has drawn up a balance-sheet of costs: "Our aggregate military capital inventory, which amounted to $20b. in 1973, had increased by fifty per cent by 1979 and another fifty per cent by 1984. Last year it reached $50b.—and this in peace time!"

Results are startling, as in the United States: inability by the army to gather and train a quantity of human brain-power large enough to make effective use of the mass of materiel piled up. Ben-Dor points out: "For lack of qualified pilots and for lack of modern training facilities, our air force has already moth-

balled 90 modern fighter-planes, out of a total
of 600, as military headquarters admits. We
need statesmanship far more than we need
further weapon purchases."

Shimon Peres thinks aloud about the whole
military concept in the age of technology.
"Wars are no longer fought for materialistic
objectives. Natural resources like oil, iron or
even gold play such a diminishing role that
they do not evoke the greed of the conqueror.
Learning and knowledge are the true raw
material. You showed me the incredible smallness of the latest, powerful computer chip.
How much material does this chip contain?
Almost none. The input it needs is knowledge.

"So what is there to fight for? Land? Not
any more. People? If they are sophisticated
they will fight back. If they are under-developed they will produce so many children that
you will have to spend your resources in
providing for them, while you become gradually and inevitably a minority.

"The real struggle in the world today
between the Communist and democratic
systems is not for the land of the people, but
for the hearts of the people, the minds of the
people.

"While the politicians on each side are eager

to convince the public that their system is the right one, their end-purpose is not any more to gain supporters outside the country. The game is to build up support inside the country. If they like to be appreciated outside, that is because it helps acceptance inside.

"Gorbachev is anxious, as was Khrushchev, to show that Russia is a success story. Reagan is anxious to show that America is strong and moving ahead. Their encounter is not a confrontation over the size of their respective lands or the wealth of their respective mineral deposits, it is a contest for the minds of the people. That is what leads them occasionally to get involved foolishly in regional wars. Think back to Algeria or Vietnam or, more recently, the Red Army in Afghanistan or the American agonies in Central America.

"The result is that more and more money goes to military budgets, away from economic development. And what can the military provide? Can they make you any wiser? Can the military add to your quality of life? There is paradoxically one thing the military can do, and that is itself a problem: it can provide you with justification for expenditure on research.

"Even that is not straightforward. It is hard to convince a nation to spend as much on research as it does on the manufacture of new missiles. People everywhere are traditionally forgiving of disbursements on military hardware, even if it is not used—even if it cannot be used, as in the case of nuclear arsenals. Research excites less interest, and as to civilian research, that is readily sacrificed—although it is designed to produce a better life! These are facts, we cannot ignore them."

He feels I remain unconvinced, so digs out of his own experience an eloquent example. "One day long ago we were visited by a promising young British leader. He came to our country and told me at a private meeting: 'I shall be prime minister.' His name was Harold Wilson. I spoke with him at length, he was an interesting man. You were at a party held in London, I remember, when he became Labour leader, and you told me you were impressed by his interest in modern technology.

"I said to him: 'Once you become prime minister, what are you going to do?' He replied: 'I am going to dismantle all military research and invest the money in civilian research. I shall stop missile development and military aircraft development. I shall devote the money saved to medicine, education, oceanography.' I cautioned him: 'Be careful, you may wind up one form of research, the military, and then discover that the trade unions will not let you spend the money on the other, the civilian research.'

"That is exactly what happened. When Labour came to power, they cut credits to the aeronautic and missile industries. But the money taken away was not used for development, it was channelled to welfare. Remember the welfare state? And Britain became smaller, not greater as an industrial power.

"I tell you this because I see today in the minds of the Americans and the Russians another new temptation: to dominate space. Do we have a simple argument to refute this new form of competition, this new 'star' attraction, this new race for conquest? I must admit I cannot suggest one.

"Taking all the above into account I don't foresee another war, but on the other hand I don't foresee any genuine, large-scale disarmament either. I fear a new rationale, a new excuse for wasting resources on another kind of bellicosity: space war. And still no priority for using funds to create a better life."

※　　　　※　　　　※

## A new kind of hero

The prodigious waste of resources by the two super-powers in their competition with each other cannot last for ever. The cost is too great, there must be a Soviet–American rapprochement. It will eventuate gradually—and so will peace, because of the present general economic debacle. The challenge to Israel in the new era is to become a knowledge factory instead of a fortress. For its own benefit and for the benefit of the whole region. The opportunity is historic.

I have just studied a collection of papers by top American scientists under the heading "The New Computer Revolution". The collection is edited and presented by the director of IBM's computer-science laboratories. His name happens to be a Hebrew one: Abraham Peled. He started his higher education at the Technion in Haifa, from which he holds a degree. He proceeded with a doctoral thesis in Princeton, USA. I tell this to Shimon Peres, to whom I had sent these texts, so that he should have first-hand knowledge of them. I read aloud some of the excerpts:

"The progress in computing systems will continue—perhaps exponentially and certainly unabated—for at least the next ten or 15 years. The widespread availability of computers to a growing community of users will improve creativity and promote continued progress. Currently computing can amplify only simple, relatively routine mental activities, but steady advance is being made towards enhancing the more analytical and inferential skills.

"Just as machines capable of extending human physical abilities created the Industrial Revolution, so computing, through its capacity to extend man's mental abilities, is the engine propelling the current historic (but as yet nameless) technological revolution. The great journey has only begun."

This Israeli, this American, this scientist, is able to take a realistic look at the breathtaking prospects of the coming years. But do we listen? Are we ready to pick up the gauntlet? Do we believe that the militaristic atmosphere of the past can be replaced by a different kind of challenge which will spark youth and the human spirit towards a new kind of excellence?

"In many ways the individual is an echo of his generation or of the public he faces," Shimon Peres answers. "Most army heroes accomplished what they did because they wanted to gain the respect of their fellow-soldiers and of the community. It is known about our forces for example that in times of danger before, during and after an emergency, we have the highest mobilization of effort. Public respect is great, and legitimately so, for people who are ready to sacrifice their lives in order to confront the danger and ward it off. When normal times return the prestige of the army goes down again, because its importance in the eyes of the public sags.

"If the people feel that science, computers and knowledge are the real hope and challenge, you will find an echo of that recognition in the minds of gifted young persons. They will react with the same zest as they show now when called for military duty.

"Required, I admit, is a radical change of values. Peace has to be endowed with the glamour that was hitherto reserved for wars of national salvation. The public has to be educated to this. Only when it understands the new order shall we have a mobilization of younger people. I think it is possible."

Israelis could become as proud of what they can do for the cause of new knowledge as they are proud of what they do now for their country's defence. When the change is made, many scientists in the world will want to

91

contribute something of their talent for Israel. But the condition is very specific: that Israel prove itself capable of switching from capacity for war to creativity for peace. Then, and only then, will these people be willingly recruited from all over. Does Shimon Peres agree?

Progress creates its own dynamic, he says. "I have gathered a group which is called 'The 100-day group', to prepare a creative structure for peace. The idea is that when you take on a problem you should only have something like a hundred days to act on it. The first hundred days are crucial, particularly in a democratic system, because when things are done in a brisk and businesslike way, there is less resentment.

"Any attempt to cut through the delays of bureaucracy is appreciated and generates new momentum. That is what I tried to do when I became prime minister. We set ourselves the hundred-day deadline to terminate the war in Lebanon and halt inflation. It worked.

"Now, to stimulate discussion one of the questions I put before the latest 100-day group was: how can we make Israel as advanced as Japan? It was immediately clear that peace is the first requirement. It was equally clear that to sit down and wait for peace is to lose time. We have to make our preparations in advance, so that when peace comes everything is organized, and the country is ready to exploit new openings.

"I heard a story that the Japanese have begun training the child even before birth, teaching him music in the womb so that as soon as he is born he is soothed by the sound of melody. The moral is that you cannot start too early. For me peace begins at the first moment of 'pregnancy', and by pregnancy I mean the minute we start negotiating.

"I feel we can draw up programmes of development and knowledge right away. The minute peace is in the womb, we can already start applying them. That is why I devote so much energy to initiating the peace-process. The negotiations when they come will of course be complicated and may take time, but the moment the meetings begin we can start to create.

"What we are also trying to do here, you and I together, is give the full picture: that peace is not a passive situation but offers creative opportunities. It is not just sitting instead of standing; it is walking instead of falling back. We want Israel to join the scientific revolution. To use your phrase, let the

93

promised land become the land of knowledge.

"What we have to do is prod people's imagination. Generation after generation has been filled with reluctance, fear and suspicion. The fence of scepticism is the first barrier; once we can overcome that we can change everything. Our task is to give substance to the future and overcome scepticism.

"The future offers promise to all of us independently. I mean we won't be imposing on each other, we are not trying to swap one dependency for another. All of us will benefit, both as individuals and collectively. In the era ahead each becomes his own master and makes his own choice."

I must share with him a topic that was brought to my attention forcibly at my latest meeting with academic people: "Yesterday in Tel Aviv university they expressed the need for a modern school of computerized management. Lack of progress in management science means a hemorrhage of resources in all fields, among them the new computing power.

"A kind of cultural revolution is going on in this field in America. It aims to redefine curricula, methods of teaching and methods of learning at the famous business schools, which have fallen behind and need up-dating.

"I find here the same preoccupation. To drop behind in management means to waste our most precious resource: brain-power."

*        *        *

On Saturdays at lunchtime our political discussions are interrupted. Peres has a particular fondness for the younger generation. He reserves every Sabbath occasion for the visit of his children and grandchildren. I watch him. He listens to them whatever their age, he enquires about their activities, he lets them express their ideas, he consults with them.

The small ones play on the carpet. Doors bang; it is a family scene. When he talks about Israel's future he is thinking of their future. After a time we move away and resume our discourse.

He finds the professors' observations about management revealing. "In human life," he says, "we differentiate between the things we have to learn and the things we are supposed to know. Maybe that distinction is wrong. We are theoretically supposed to know how to eat, how to breathe, how to sleep; but I am not sure that we are really so well briefed. The only thing we believe we really have to learn is how to work. Living is presumed to be instinctive. And so is administration.

"Lack of proper attention to the subject of administration leads to an enormous waste of resources, it leads in fact to bureaucracy. I have seen it happen, I know it in my bones. We must recognize that here is this vast domain, administration, which costs us half our wealth. How to handle it, how to rationalize it, how to computerize it? We must not wait.

"Administration was introduced as an organized activity by the military. It is the domain 'par excellence' where civilians have learned from the army: hierarchy, discipline, line of command. The civilians invented democracy, but the military invented administration.

"Among the very first to understand the crucial need for good management was Moses. Though the leader of the Jewish people, he was a very poor administrator. He didn't know how to 'manage' the community. So he invited a foreign expert by the name of Jethro, who came to teach him how to organize. Jethro said: you must appoint a head for every thousand people, a head for every hundred people, a head for every ten people. You must appoint judges and organize a police force.

Then Moses was able, still in the desert, to guide his marching people efficiently towards their destiny. That is the first reference in literature to the art of administration."

Peres's reluctance to rely on man's native instinct and his preference for intellectual reflection reminded me of an essay on nature by the poet Charles Baudelaire. He writes: "Nature teaches nothing. It pushes man to kill his peers, to sequester their possessions, to torture them.... Fine and noble things derive from reason, from thinking problems out."

Peace does not come naturally, it has to be contrived. I take this up with Peres: "Of all the artifacts that the human brain can create, the most precious, the most delicate, is peace. If Israel harnesses its brainpower, imagination and creativity to forging peace, it will achieve something superior. If not, everything that Israel does is undermined.

"We need peace not only for ourselves," he reminds me. "We want to remain Jewish and democratic, so we have to answer Palestinian aspirations and not only our own. Peace means considering also the demands of the other party. We have to go half-way or at least part of the way towards the other side. I believe we should not look upon peace stati-

cc-g

cally, as a static development, but as something dynamic. I feel that the most crucial point today is to start negotiating. If we had reached the stage of negotiation earlier we might have been spared the recent Arab disturbances. They stemmed from the feeling that all roads are blocked.

"The minute you start moving, the movement itself becomes important. Let us not introduce into our peace process anything which might block the road. That includes, surprisingly enough, ready-made plans, because any plan I might make will not be acceptable to the Arabs; and the other way round. We must do everything we can to get the talks launched, and once we start negotiation, only then should we introduce supportive ideas.

"We want to solve the problems earnestly and sincerely, so we must be single-minded and say: let us start peace talks without qualifications, without conditions attached. Peace is not just the end of war, it is the beginning of a new and constructive relationship. That must be our obsession.

"This is where the new sciences should really help. Modern science is anti-border, anti-frontier, it is indivisible.

## A new kind of hero

*"Today everybody must belong to two enti-*
*ties, the entity of the nation and the entity of*
*knowledge.* The former has borders and frontiers, the latter does not. The former has
memories, the latter has potential. They are
two different worlds. Poetically I would say
that for the first time we can live on earth and
in heaven. We shall belong to the heaven of
knowledge, while remaining the residents of a
divided world."

# 6

# The land of tomorrow

The new "wealth of nations" no longer rests on an accumulation of factories, but on a steady deepening of knowledge. Scientists support this reversal of priorities, but are reluctant to seek political influence. Politicians are kept chained by a fearful conservatism to the misguided old equation: robots equal unemployment.

President Reagan launched his re-election campaign with the words: "America is back, standing strong!" People wanted to believe him. Since then disappointments have been inflicted by the rising power of Japan.

Moreover Japan, far from being a unique case, is part of an ever growing East Asian economy. Washington announced in February: "The administration will put an end, as of January 1989, to the preferential customs treatment accorded so far by the United States to four 'developing countries' of South-East

Asia—Taiwan, Singapore, Korea and Hong Kong."

Thus ends the remarkable adventure of a free-trade zone between America and the four "tigers", which has proved so beneficial over the last twenty years, at least to the emerging Asian nations.

This common market for products, investments, factories and capital, which brought the American market to the western shores of the Pacific, has redressed a traditional imbalance. The four small countries have by their own efforts surged from the abyss of under-development. They did that by automating their factories and training human brains. Their combined trade surplus with the US now exceeds that of Japan.

Their products will therefore be charged customs at the US border in order to slow down their intimidating penetration of the American market. This follows on the use of import quotas to brake the inroads of Japanese industry. The reasons are the same: products from Asia have become cheaper and better than their American counterparts. Hence the tariffs, the barriers, the protectionism.

But it did not work, protectionism never does. Japanese industrialists reacted to the new barriers against their entry by putting up factories of their own (with computerized systems and training programmes) right inside the United States, where they can now penetrate the market from within, more effectively than before.

The decline of the dollar versus the yen has paradoxically increased the financial power of Japanese banks which, together with their corporate clients, are pushing their domination into the very heart of Wall Street. Thus protectionism has brought an effect opposite to that intended—an intensification of the Japanese penetration. The hold of the Japanese has become all but impregnable. Their research and production centres, sub-contractor chains and commercial networks are spread all over the United States. The Japanese economy employs today so many Americans—American voters—that the issue has become delicate indeed.

What the Asian countries have accomplished is not a miracle, but a sophisticated use of human resources. Singapore has grasped the fact that intellect is the key raw material in the new global economy. Its universities were built up, and two strategic decisions were taken by the political leadership:

1. All factories must be automated, and then all the services computerized.
2. The whole population must be educated in computer literacy.

Not content with copying Japan, Singapore has advanced further. Like Taiwan it now exports to Japan itself. Predictably, Japanese industrial firms together with American ones are establishing laboratories of their own in Singapore.

٭          ٭          ٭

I spend time in Jerusalem today because here lives, as we have seen, one of the few Western leaders who have realized the critical significance of the computer breakthrough. The only other similarly enlightened states-man that I have talked to is François Mitterrand.

I had the privilege to work on this topic with Mitterrand. We were impeded by burdens from the past. The heavy fortress of "national education", centralized in Paris, had resisted every attempt at reform. It did not budge even though the country's youth were seriously disturbed, seeing their own future threatened. The situation is still unresolved, the strife continues.

## The land of tomorrow

Shimon Peres has come to Paris on a number of occasions since 1980, and it was in Paris that he realized the importance of the knowledge revolution and of its computer tools for Israel's renewal.

In 1985, as head of the Computer Literacy Centre in Paris, I was completing three years of close cooperation with a world authority, Raj Reddy of Carnegie-Mellon University. He had agreed to become scientific director of the French centre, dividing his time between that and his professorship in Pittsburgh (where he heads the world's first Robotics Institute).

Thanks to him we were able to create ties between, on the one hand, a number of important French schools, including the three national polytechnic institutes (Grenoble, Nancy and Toulouse), and on the other hand, the Carnegie-Mellon consortium of universities. In late 1985 I was asked to chair the International Committee of Carnegie-Mellon.

François Mitterrand wanted to be the first head of state to visit our Pittsburgh campus. He delivered a major address there on the computer era, and awarded the Legion of Honour to Raj Reddy. Last year Shimon Peres, soon after leaving the post of prime minister, made an official visit to Carnegie-Mellon, and spent a day at the Robotics Institute.

He met and talked with the leaders of the university, headed by the president Richard M. Cyert. An arrangement had been negotiated similar to the one embracing the French institutes, adding five Israeli universities to the link-up with the American consortium. Peres confirmed approval of this cooperation agreement, thus building a foundation for creative interaction among scientists.

There was a moment of spontaneous dialogue in the university between Shimon Peres and Professor Herbert Simon, Nobel prize-winner in economics and founder of the field of artificial intelligence.

*Herbert Simon:*—In understanding the human brain we should be able to better our methods of education and stimulate intellectual creativity. We took our ideas to Beijing, China, where we planned to build a three-year curriculum, using a system based on learning from examples. Result: the students who participated not only did better than the others, they finished their work in two years instead of three. Now we are starting a similar experiment with Americans.

*Shimon Peres*:—How can we use this new insight?

*Simon*:—We think we can arrange a computer curriculum that does its own teaching. So here is an application: use the computer to better understand our own learning mechanisms.

Next we say maybe computers can simulate human thought. It will be startling to discover that machines can carry out thinking processes. That leads us to wonder whether we are justified in seeing human beings as unique. We have to think about how we men fit into the larger scheme of things. The problem is not how we separate ourselves from nature but how we unite with it. We must look at ourselves in relation to a much larger world and learn how to live at peace with that world.

*Peres*:—You say that this technology will soon be available in two new domains, teaching and decision-making.

*Simon*:—Yes, in fact such expert systems are already being used on a large scale. Decision-making computers are widely employed in industry, thus saving time and permitting human personnel to devote their attention to other things.

*Peres*:—Can the computer foretell the

consequences of a person's own decisions? Can it make better judgments than the human mind?

*Simon*:—Only if there is a valid theory in the field. If an engineer designs a motor he can tell you pretty well how it will operate. So can the computer. But if someone tells you that you should follow a particular economic policy, neither the economist nor the computer can do a very good job of predicting what will happen. For the theory, as you know, is not there.

*Peres*:—The reason is simple: economics depends a great deal on psychology. People's expectations are subjective, and no computer can predict subjective expectations, even about the economic future.

*Simon*:—Recent developments in mathematics, now reaching the press, lead us to be a little pessimistic about our ability to predict things even in the field of pure logic. There is now a so-called theory of chaos, which shows that mathematical systems too can behave unpredictably.

*Peres*:—Fascinating. Well, after listening to this we may not be blamed for becoming more sceptical.

*Simon*:—Maybe in some areas.

# The land of tomorrow

*     *     *

On the day following this encounter, before his return to Jerusalem, I interrogated Shimon Peres about the applicability of what he had heard to the economic development of Israel and the Middle East.

"First of all," he answers, "the thing you call 'computer literacy' has paramount importance. I feel as if I was in the age of Gutenberg after he invented the printing press five centuries ago. Gutenberg enabled one person to communicate with many, now the process is vastly accelerated. We have an entirely new vehicle which can master whole worlds of information, communication, calculation.

"What impressed me most was how the new science meets up with philosophy. This was put very well by Herbert Simon. His quest is for levels of achievement that nobody can yet reach. Once we understand—through developments in computer science, artificial intelligence and cognitive science—how the brain operates, we shall have the secret of a new world.

"The brain's unique power is not its learning capacity nor its memory capacity, but its capacity to create. Albert Camus (the French author born in Algeria) wrote that there is just one essential issue and that is suicide. Without presuming to dispute his ideas, I think personally that the problem is not dying. The problem is living, and using life for creative purposes.

"It is easy to die, it is difficult to live creatively. It is difficult to conceive how to build a human world. In a very soft voice I would say that there is indeed an intractable question facing us in these times, tangled as we are in the technicalities of the machine age. The question is how to make these complicated devices serve our true purpose, which is: the achievement of the good life.

"The second thing I learnt is the large part played in all domains by preparations for the human activity next in line. Scientists think how to construct, with their new scientific tools, an even more advanced computer scheme over the next two decades. The third point I have noted is how dangerous it is to wait, to lag behind.

"The final lesson is the need to come down to earth, the obligation to make immediate innovations.

"Most of us are impatient, but we cannot

have any real break-through without what Professor Simon calls the necessary 'maturing years'. One needs a formative period to become a pianist, to become a painter, to learn a language, to qualify as a scientist. Learning starts like in a desert. You go in a desert, it doesn't have buildings, it doesn't have water wells or anything you recognize. You plod on and you think it is endless and hopeless. But if you are determined you reach an oasis, and you discover the promised land."

*                *                *

In computers even the most sophisticated hardware accounts for no more than 15 or 20 per cent of the cost, the rest is software. Experts in large numbers are still needed for making software programmes, the work involved can be described as labour-intensive. Israel does not have anything like enough qualified people for the job—nobody has. So study is now devoted to "software engineering": how to manufacture software without putting too many people on it.

This is a new branch of technology and it can be started in Israel. A federal Software Engineering Institute exists in the US, and there will not be another over the next five years. Japan does not have even one. Koji Kobayashi, chairman of NEC, the large electronics company, complained about that during a session last summer in Tokyo, and sent his scientists to visit the American installation.

Another important new development attracting people and investments is the American technological "complex": a university with a strong science faculty, surrounded by an industrial park. Corporate laboratories draw on the theoretical work done in the university. The complex is based on a common pool of trained brains. This is the cradle of the future economy.

The heart and engine of Silicon Valley is Stanford University. High-tech industries wanted to be nearby and to share in the innovative talent of this great academy. That was the origin of the "valley". The same happened in New England round the famous universities of Harvard and MIT. Today New England enjoys the lowest level of unemployment in the US, less than 3 per cent—thanks to this faculty-factory symbiosis. (Not surprisingly Massachusetts was the launching pad for Mike Dukakis's campaign of renewal.)

The same process has started now in western Pennsylvania around Carnegie-Mellon.

This university has decided to follow the logic of the computer revolution to the limit. Professor Richard Cyert, its president, the most innovative economist, came to two fundamental conclusions:

1. A modern university has to be totally computerized. Each active member (professor, researcher, student) must possess his own personal computer. All must be linked through a network to the various data-banks and other institutes on campus.

2. A modern university carries an overriding national responsibility. It cannot be just a centre of learning; the ivory-tower role is a thing of the past. Universities must help modernize industry and make it competitive. They have become an integral part of the production process, being as they are in charge of a critical input in the modern economy, the input of knowledge.

Shimon Peres wanted to know in detail how the business corporations, those cells of America's economic life, respond to the stimulation of their propinquity to institutes of higher education. He was given a variety of examples illustrating how major undertakings, under the pressure of Asian competition, have been drawn over the last five years into

CC-H

this kind of cooperation. Some put up laboratories in the complex's industrial park, others sign contracts of "regular consultations" with top specialists at the university.

Carnegie-Mellon has such connections with Westinghouse, IBM, Digital, General Motors, Ford, Lockheed, American Express. Many others join each month, as do international enterprises like Siemens (Germany), Volvo (Sweden), Aerospatiale (France), Hitachi and NEC (Japan). The above companies are mentioned because of their magnitude, and the fact that they possess all kinds of research centres of their own, since they can afford the investment. Yet they see the need for direct ties with the fertile brain-pool of the university. This is still a new phenomenon.

Such is the tissue of the modern economic world. The pressures of competition create strange bedfellows. Shimon Peres named his visit: "A voyage to the world of tomorrow." He took many personal notes and we discussed his conclusions.

"The road ahead is clear," he tells me, "and I know that Israel is made for this. The reason is simple: our only natural resource is our human beings. They are the driving force of progress. Machines can be produced anywhere, but human models are more diffi-cult to come by. We must focus our efforts on the excellence of our people.

"I remember that President Sadat once asked me why kibbutzim are so successful in agriculture. My reply was that this is the first serious attempt to apply the principles of the cooperative movement in agriculture. The resulting team-work obviates the need for a costly and burdensome administration.

"Whatever we do in life, half of it goes to pay for management. This is surely anachron-istic. I think that both capitalism and socialism have discovered their common enemy: bureaucracy.

"I don't know if people have lost their trust in the Supreme Being, but they have certainly lost their trust in highly-placed private per-sons. There is a pervasive revolt against governments, against bureaucracy, against the dominance of structure. The feeling has spread that freedom is decentralization, that freedom is not only freedom of expression, but the capacity to make your own decisions. You are free not when you merely speak, but when you also decide. Every reform that enables you to decide important things by yourself contains the seeds of real democracy.

"The closer the gap between the decision-makers and the people, the better society will become. The computer revolution enables a lot of individuals to join the higher order because they have a prime instrument for decision-making, which is: information. No matter how much intuition you are endowed with there is an asset you cannot do without—maximal and pertinent information.

"The small computer comes into your house and says: 'Sir, if you want to make a decision, the following is the necessary knowledge and you can have it instantly.' The instrument is there, the wisdom is to collect the information, put it to use and translate it for the satisfaction of human needs. Access to these benefits can be made available in every place and at every spot.

"That is my conclusion: if Israel wants to be in the first rank of modern technology it must organize itself around the optimal use of information. Any country doing that has a great advantage.

"The second conclusion that comes to mind about this new computer era is that we are witnessing the end of mass-production and the beginning of production by small units able to tap a mass of knowledge and expertise.

"If you take a piece of land it is no longer its size that determines the production of vegetables and fruits, but the knowledge invested in its cultivation. This is important in our relation with the Arabs. Let me put the matter another way. It is not how many dunams or hectares you own, but how much knowledge you own.

"The third point: what struck me more than the miniaturization of the machine is the miniaturization of the investment. The amount of capital required is so modest that it can be available to practically every industry, every town, every school—to everyone.

"It is said that Ford generated a greater revolution than Lenin because he made a vehicle available to each individual. By doing that he turned every producer into a consumer. Here we have the 'Second Industrial Revolution'. Today we must take the lead into a still newer era of science, where the wealth of people is based on knowledge. The requisite for investment decisions now is not the possession of finance but the possession of a scientific idea with a technological application. It is amazing how low the actual monetary cost is, and how great is the revolution."

He focusses on essential targets for the coming effort. "The place to start is the schools. The dominating discipline of all disciplines, the dominant effort of all efforts, is education.

"*Gorky used to say: 'My life is my university'. Soon we shall be saying: 'The university is my life'.* Each person in modern times must understand that education begins with the first air that he breathes, the first glance he has of the world; and it will not stop until his last breath. If we want to be up-to-date education will no longer cease at the age of 18 or 21, it is becoming a continuous and dynamic process.

"My concluding remark is that technology has created a myth. When I receive a visiting personality in the Foreign Ministry, the subject that keeps cropping up is high technology. People feel intuitively that the fate of their country depends on that. Whether they know about it in detail or not, they sense that here is the path they must tread.

"We thus find a new avenue of relationship with the Arab countries. The sharing of knowledge with them at this stage may seem to many as premature and therefore irrelevant. I look on it as providing a real advantage. We have to propose it because that is what people are looking for. We can't offer an Arab farmer the same parcel of soil to cultivate with us, but in times of peace we can offer an Arab neighbour the same parcel of knowledge to cultivate with us."

"I find it very encouraging," I interceded, "that your foreign visitors speak as you said. Of course the obstacles, the rigidities, are many. In every society there is a strong conservative reflex against change, especially if change is rapid. This is also true, I notice, in Israel.

"When you chaired our workshop in Jerusalem last July (on the computer link-up with Carnegie-Mellon), there were leading members present from the universities, from the army, from industry. I remember how after two or three hours of discussion you suddenly said: 'Gentlemen, when I hear you I ask myself: am I the youngest of you all? You sound so conservative, so mistrusting.'

"I realized that even in this country of pioneers one has to push; which leads to a thought. Maybe your task is no longer to lead a party with all its bureaucracy, its rivalries, its platitudes. Why not turn over a new leaf? Perhaps you should address yourself to your young public in Israel. Once the young understand the potential and are mobilized, they will mobilize others.

"As a political leader speaking to adults you face not only the barriers of ideology or partisanship, but the scepticism, the fear of technology and change. Youth are different, they carry the will to forge a different future."

These remarks led me to an intriguing thought: "I see your task ahead as being similar in many ways to the task that Gandhi took on with the Indian people—his massive people, his passive people. He had to convince them of something important, that they could do better than import everything from England, including all their clothing, all their tools. That they were capable of manufacturing these things by themselves.

"Remember, he started this self-help process at his own initiative by taking salt from the sea. Later he weaved new fabrics with his own hands. The examples he set were telling each Indian: you can do much more than you think you can. He started a social revolution.

"You could do the same, Shimon Peres. You have now installed a personal computer in your office, on your desk. Your work is thus made more productive, even more human. Well you can go further, your work in

your office is just the first step. Adapting
Gandhi's example to the present age you
could become a computerized leader, with all
the information and knowledge at your personal disposal at any time, demonstrating to
others in all walks of life that it can be done."

# 7

# Make the desert bloom

I had numerous opportunities to travel across the arid and treeless, yet luminous Negev. It extends from Beersheba south to the Gulf of Akaba, from the long Jordanian border on the east to the Egyptian border on the west. The Negev desert covers nearly two-thirds of Israel's territory. I return there once more. We know now that human intelligence and the application of the latest technology can transform the Negev into another California.

"Even if the place appears at first a little hostile," Peres had told me, "*we would rather master the hostility of a land than the hatred of a population.*"

The pioneer future of Israel lies in the south, as its first prime minister, David Ben-Gurion, declared. He made his home during his latter days in Sde Boker, midway between Jerusalem and the Red Sea. He expressed his desire to be buried in that spot, it was his last will and testament.

So I went back to the Negev, Ben-Gurion university, the Desert Institute, the Dimona Research Centre, the kibbutz at Sde Boker. And I found not only the striking beauty of wild nature, but also the devotion of men and women who have chosen to dwell and work in that stark south. Here lies the spirit of Israel. Far away from racial disturbances and political disputes, facing the permanent challenge of a seemingly desolate nature with its untapped resources.

Shimon Peres, to whom I brought a comforting report, confirmed his keen interest in this frontierland. "Yes, I do believe the Negev, together with Galilee in the north, should be a top Israeli priority over the years to come. It is half our territory—and it's empty. Whatever we do there will clash, not with the hostility of a people but only with the hostility of nature. It calls for the pioneering spirit, the enterprise of a young generation to build something new and different.

"This desert stretch could be the focal point for our relations both with Jordan and Egypt, because our frontiers with both countries—in the Negev zone—are well-defined and accepted. The one exception is our dispute with Egypt, now under negotiation, over the ownership of Taba, a particle of land one square mile in size, containing a smart hotel. The rest of the Negev's borders are not only unquestioned, they are even unfenced.

"The area has possibilities in many fields: energy, irrigation, the exploitation of the Dead Sea, transport, tourism, and science in all its aspects. The call here is for forward thinking and initiative. A good plan could arouse the enthusiasm of everybody concerned with the Negev."

I have recently read in a book of memoirs this evocation by Shimon Peres of his first prime minister: "Ben-Gurion decided to quit the government in December 1953. He had always been attracted by the Negev, he saw in it Israel's greatest land reservoir.

"He encouraged the colonization of the desert, the Negev had a special charm for him. Sde Boker, placed as it was on the surface of the moon, at the heart of this big circle of mountains, conjured up a vision of the infinite possibilities that lie ahead. For Ben-Gurion, the location symbolized the biblical genesis. He went there to accelerate what had been started."

At the latest World Sephardi Congress Peres added this remark: "The Promised Land

4,000 years after Moses is not just a known land, it can become a land of knowledge. It may be poor in natural resources, but that no longer matters. We live at a time when riches can be encapsulated in a chip so small as to be almost invisible, like a cell of the brain. We, the Jewish people, were born for this age."

A quotation from the Bible that I saw engraved on the front of Ben-Gurion University, "The desert shall rejoice and blossom as the rose", reminded me of a request that Raj Reddy had made to me when I was leaving the United States. Raj said: "Tell Shimon we'll make the desert bloom." That is his vision as an Indian villager who rose to be a master of the new sciences.

Twenty years ago when I was researching for my first book, *The American Challenge*, I found a quotation from Jean Jaures, the French socialist leader who was assassinated at the opening of the First World War, because of his passion for peace. Jaures said: "Finally everything proceeds from the human mind. Even things that we think derive from nature, like bread and wine, are in truth marvellous human artifacts."

These were my thoughts while journeying through the desiccated south. On my return I

126

asked Peres: "Why does Israel seem indifferent to its real frontier, to the Negev?"

He said: "Over the last ten years since the Likud party won office in the elections, they have put before our young generation the requirement to make their homes not in the Negev, but in the heart of the West Bank and in Gaza. It is a political, not an agricultural, type of settlement. It is not settling on the land but staking ownership over territories and people.

"The settlers do not generally become farmers, they are overnight residents who spend the day working elsewhere. Furthermore the bulk of the territories are densely populated by Arabs, and that is a problem. Human beings are unbreakable eggs, you cannot make them into omelets. When Arab and Jewish people live together, that does not turn them into a community. The conflict remains.

"We were always opposed to creating settlements in the heavily-inhabited Arab areas, because we felt that it would aggravate the existing clash and we wanted to keep all options open. Moreover the deflection of settlers to such problematic areas meant that the Negev and up to a point the Galilee would be ignored. Thousands of young people were actually led to move out of the Negev, shifting their homes to the West Bank and Gaza. A terrible error of judgment.

"For our part we shall be offering the young generation the challenge of the Negev instead of the challenge of the West Bank and Gaza. Facing a shortage of budgetary funds we have to concentrate on essentials. We cannot do everything at once and the first priority should be given to the Negev and Galilee.

"I said jokingly to Gush Emunim, the ones who chose to settle in the West Bank, that the trouble with the Negev is that there are not enough Arabs there. They appear to be looking for Arabs, that is their challenge. The problem with Israel's southern region is that it hasn't got a lobby.

"The industrialized parts of the country are by definition a vested interest; a hubbub of voices speak for them. A good leader should represent the needs of tomorrow. He should speak for the unrepresented and should invest effort in them. He should not yield to the pressures of today, the audiences of today.

"A simple example: you cannot develop the Negev without building an infra-structure of roads, railways and small airstrips, because people feel more tranquil if they can easily reach the centre of the country.

"But the big cities of Israel face terrible traffic congestion. What should the government do? Should we invest all our money in eliminating the traffic jam round Tel Aviv and Haifa? Or should we spend less there in order to improve our communications with the Negev? A balance must be struck between the areas that are congested today and those that may, if we are not careful, become congested tomorrow.

"In the last budget I asked the finance minister to allocate a small amount of $50m. for the Negev's infra-structure. I took it upon myself to release money from other sources, because the minister said he didn't have any spare cash.

"We are told that roads create an economy; the truth is that they also create culture. When you construct a good road you create an opening for civilization. If you want to develop a place, pave the way for development."

He points at a large map and proceeds to draw three lines on it. He explains:

"One: this goes from sea to sea, from the Mediterranean in the west to the Red Sea in

CC-I

129

the south. It extends along the frontier between Egypt and ourselves. The frontier is a straight line, cut officially after the First World War, as soon as the British took over. A recently-built highway runs along it, linking the Mediterranean (where we have quite a large city, Ashkelon) to Eilat.

"Two: Another frontier in the east, from the Dead Sea to the Red Sea. We ought to reach an agreement with the Jordanians over a canal we want to build, linking the two coasts. It will raise the level of the Dead Sea and we must get Jordanian consent to that. There is a plan. Because of differences in altitude there will be a hydro-electric power-station. It should cost us something like $1.5b. to cut this kind of canal, but it will change the face of the district, which is today dry and barren. Two artificial lakes will form a reservoir of solar energy. It will take two to four years, depending on the technology.

"The mountains on the Jordanian side are higher. When clouds move in the skies they don't stop on our side, and most of the rain falls in Jordan. It is wasted there because it does not fall on cultivated land. We estimate that 300 cubic metres of totally sweet water pours into the Dead Sea, for no good use.

"We are short of water as you know, so we try to hunt the clouds before they get to Jordan, using artificial means. We shoot mercury injections at them. Requisitioning this precious fluid would help the Jordanians as well as us, it is a treasure in this dry area. Their share could be used for irrigation or whatever they want, which is an added advantage of the plan.

"Alongside the Arava, a valley linking the two seas, we already have more than 15 agricultural villages (kibbutzim and moshavim). We would like to double their number. This is the site I have in mind for a high-tech kibbutz on Raj Reddy's model. Some of the villages are outstanding in their beauty and success. One is called Ein Gedi, an oasis in the desert. Further south near Eilat is Yotvata, a kibbutz which lives on dairy products, selling the best ice-cream in the country. Almost all its members are top-grade technicians with university degrees.

"South of Ein Gedi stands the Sapir Centre for Technology. Nearby we are going to build the Voice of America radio station, a $300m. investment. Some of our people will criticize me over this. Now that there is a rapprochement between the Americans and the Russians, they say, why build a station? Well, why not? If there is a rapprochement, the Voice of America can send nice messages to the Soviet Union. Who says all messages must be aggressive?

"Next we intend to build a railroad. We also plan to put up one of the largest solar energy stations there is, in Eilat. It is a technique based on a set of mirrors which catch the rays of the sun at the most efficient moment, using an automatic computer. The computer follows the movement of the sun. In the morning the computer opens its eyes with the first ray. It moves the mirror so as to catch the maximum heat of the sun and transform it into electricity. The station will produce something like 60 megawatts; and that is only a beginning.

"Three: Dominating the north of the Negev we have a full-blown town which is Beersheba, and around Beersheba we want to build a major industrial complex. There is a beginning of it, and an airfield.

"Mitzpe Ramon, isolated in the heart of the desert (not far from Sde Boker), did not take off. We want to save it. It sits magnificently on the rim of a giant natural crater. We are going to build in Mitzpe Ramon a centre for the arts.

*Make the desert bloom*

"That is how we see the beginning of this exotic zone: a flourishing agriculture competitive in world markets, a canal, a railroad, a chain of new kibbutzim, the industrial centre, the university in Beersheba, and tourism.

"Let us not forget that, as I said, this is the part of the country which borders on our two most important neighbours: Jordan and Egypt. The population of Jordan, estimated at 3m., is two-thirds Palestinian. There are many overlapping matters on which joint consideration is possible by the three neighbouring countries, Egypt, Jordan and Israel."

For more than an hour I had been listening as Shimon Peres, in front of large maps, talked of his plans. He was in his element. For the first time in a month I saw him liberated from practical preoccupations. His voice, his pace, his fervour are no longer those of a party chairman, or the vice-premier of a government he is not free to lead. He sounds forty years younger. He is again the ardent Zionist pioneer seized with ideas and ideals, confident in the power of his people to create a country of intelligence and science; to build the promised land.

\*　　　\*　　　\*

*The Chosen and the Choice*

Among the eminent Carnegie-Mellon professors is Akram Midani, Dean of Fine Arts.
He was born in Syria, an Arab country
bordering on Israel in the north. Possessed of
a mind encompassing the entire globe, he
seeks to effect a grand synthesis between art
and technology.

That evening I re-read a text where Midani
describes how exciting and fulfilling in human
terms the future might be. I found profound
similarities between the thought of Akram the
Arab and Shimon the Jew.

*"Art and technology," writes Midani, "had
always walked hand in hand until, at the
beginning of the 19th Century, the romantic
notion emerged of the genius as an individual.
Until then artists throughout the centuries had
worked in teams, each member a master of his
own technique. The great pyramids, the
mosques, the cathedrals were built by groups
of people banded together. They were all,
including those having the calibre of a
Leonardo da Vinci or a Michelangelo,
primarily technicians.*

*"The artificial separation between art and
science was the result, I maintain, of an intellectual error. It was believed that in serious
scholarly matters there can be no place or time*

134

*for play. Scientists and technicians thought of artists as irrational beings governed by the mysterious forces of inspiration alone. Victim of this meaningless debate has been the unity of man himself. Charles Baudelaire taught us how 'everything that is aesthetically beautiful is above all the result of exact calculation'.*

*"Computer technology magnifies the inventive power of the craftsman. That is where artists and scientists meet. Many other changes await us if we can use our new tools of knowledge to expand this re-discovered unity."*

## 8

## Lack of vision, not of talent

The Israeli economy was launched at its very beginnings eighty years ago by kibbutzim. Without capital or training, would-be farmers faced a waste land starved of rainfall for the bulk of the year. In order all the same to extract produce from their inhospitable soil they formed egalitarian village communities where they worked for no pay, all earnings accruing to the collective.

In the course of time they succeeded—perhaps too well, managing (with the aid of other types of agricultural community) to over-produce. They started therefore to diversify, assigning part of their work-force to manufacturing industrial goods.

"That departure was keenly resisted," Peres recalls. The Zionist vision spelled a return to the soil. The Jews had been 'Luftmenschen' too long. The original kibbutzniks believed fervently that they must till the earth, other occupations were disdained.

"They were right at the time, but it could not last. The division between farmer and industrialist became unnatural," says Peres. "You cannot have one part of society depending entirely upon the vagaries of wind and weather, while another lives exclusively indoors among machines. Best is a combination of all profitable activities. The new economy should unite within a single village industry, agriculture and services."

"Thus if one branch is weakened, whether because of climatic irregularities or changes in fashion, other branches are there to support it. The village community is not left to hang in the air. Kibbutzim are interesting from that point of view: over 50 per cent of their output is industrial by now, while they continue at the same time to cultivate the land as before. With the passage of time services will be added, like informatics and tourism.

"I started my working life on a kibbutz in the Valley of Jezreel, called Geva. For ideological reasons it insisted on agriculture and manual work only. Whoever didn't toil from early in the morning, when the sun rises up, to late at night well after it has set, was considered a sinner.

"Having my own ideas I suggested to Kibbutz Geva that we introduce industry. I was condemned out of hand, they almost excommunicated me. The idea was that we have to cultivate the land and nothing else. So I worked in the fields and occasionally milked the cows.

"When many years later I became Transport Minister the problem arose of damaged telephone booths. Irritated by the shortage of coins, vandals were wreaking their vengeance on the installation. In Paris I saw the magnetic card you use in the subway, and thought perhaps we could adapt it to our public telephone system.

"I wrote to the railway authority in Paris asking whether they could manufacture the device for us. We can, they answered, but not all the manufacturing is done in France, part is done outside the country. Can you tell me where? Their answer: in Kibbutz Geva.

I couldn't believe my ears. I took my car and went to the kibbutz. At the place where I used to milk cows I found an electronics complex where they produced the magnetic card for the French. You see, things don't stand still.

"The kibbutz," pursued Peres, "is the most advanced social model because it combines the

139

highest degree of freedom with the highest degree of equality. Until now both the big systems, capitalism and communism, sacrificed one of the two virtues. Here you have a community which does not have to make a choice between freedom and equality, but can enjoy both. The place is run like an Athenian democracy, with decisions taken by the assembly of all members.

"As a result of this synthesis the kibbutzim undergo very little bureaucracy. In a land which is dry and poor they have developed as good an agriculture as anywhere on earth. They are pioneers still, yet give a high place to education. Their children all complete secondary school, and some are sent from there to the universities.

"In due course they became victims of their own success, because their increasing agricultural productivity brought them to the point where they do not have employment for all their members. Machines are taking over. The irrigation of cotton in Israel, for example, is done by computer; the distribution of water is controlled by isotopes. Automatic adjustments are made for summer and winter and off-season. Fortunately the spare labour was absorbed in new industrial and other activities. That process must continue.

٭      ٭      ٭

His vision is not aimed at the distant future, he thinks of tomorrow. Where can a pilot project be launched of the new society? Among existing sectors, the one which is least rigid in its attitudes and has the greatest labour mobility is precisely the kibbutz. *Peres asked Raj Reddy to prepare plans for what the two of them nicknamed the "high-tech kibbutz".*

A small community in any environment must be able, says Reddy, to meet its own needs in terms of agriculture, industry, health and education. He has prepared plans for a "micro-factory" which, with its computer power, can supersede the familiar forms of mass-production. He also plans a "micro-university" where computers, data-banks, video disks and telecommunications can provide a small community with the best information facilities available anywhere.

He drew up a calendar for this transformation. First, the kibbutz has to be linked to the inter-university computer network, so that it can share information and knowledge. Then it must bring into play Raj Reddy's micro-factory plan. Farming too must be computerized.

Originally Israel's agriculture was based, as in all countries, on the family holding. Later each settlement chose to till a limited number of crops, achieving economies of scale.

Under Reddy's scheme crops can be grown on a small scale once more, as the old days—but much more economically this time. Programmed cultivation will permit two or three harvests a year, enabling each settlement (if it wishes) to become self-sufficient in food.

And not only food. Solar power, captured and stored by computerized solar banks, can make the kibbutz self-sufficient in energy. Within five to ten years each settlement could become an autonomous unit, self-supporting and self-sufficient, depending only marginally on external purchases or, for that matter, external sales.

Reddy's proposals imply a radical change. Village communities will be able to remove themselves from the urban orbit with which their trading needs still connect them. They can shake themselves altogether free from the "asphalt jungle".

Shimon Peres is attracted by the proposed reform. It involves, he says, a number of radical experiments: "The first requirement is to see whether we can go from mass-production to mini-production. It would be a revolution.

"The second is to see if we can shrink our dependence on traditional raw materials. Third, can we create an economic entity which combines agriculture, industry, higher studies and the selective accumulation of data in the same complex? This would be a major landmark on the way to greater local autonomy.

"The process of miniaturization may get us over one of the worst diseases of modern society: bureaucracy. The smaller, the more compact the cell you create, the less bureaucracy. Working people can be saved from their subordination to unknown, far-away decision-makers, who can be quite arbitrary, and who often don't really care."

He remains silent for a while, then asks himself: "The question is, does that look beyond the realm of reason? I don't know, but it need not take us long to find out. Within five years we would know what kind of transformation the high-tech kibbutz undergoes. So I would give it a try. Raj is a visionary, but a wise one. His head is not in the clouds.

"As I see it his plan offers a new dimension to the collective settlements. It helps them preserve the structure of this unique human

143

institution. It solves not only an economic problem, but a social one too. Some people maintain that cooperative ideas are obsolete and that only private ownership works in the modern world. The computerization of the kibbutz will prove them wrong.

"The science revolution will permit people to live differently, to develop a closer human partnership, to maintain total democracy and total equality while coping with the exigencies of modern technology. The experiment goes beyond the limits of a small industry or research activity. Achieved is a meeting of the spirit of freedom and equality with the most advanced forms of automation. If this is a success the kibbutz will not ony deal successfully with high tech, high tech will become part of the character and life of the kibbutz."

He adds: "Raj Reddy is really a rare mind. He has what I would call the talent of the horizon where sky meets earth. This man stands at the height of heavenly science, and tries to bring his vision down to daily use on earth; and with unlimited optimism.

"Usually erudition separates the thinker from life. Here you have a scientist who, in spite of his grasp of the theoretic disciplines, remains confidently pragmatic. He seems to

embody a rare combination of American curi-
osity and Indian melancholy. He gazes upon
all this American wealth at the corporate top,
yet remembers the poverty derived from
peasant cultivation of the soil in his native
land.

"My God, where is the link between the
two extremes? Raj's grasp of both make his
intellectual approach universal. I have never
seen him take sides during a discussion, he
always looks for a synthesis that will meet the
needs of all parties. This call which is not for
competition, but for coordination in a scientific community looks like an impossibility,
but it will be necessary in the coming world."

"Is there any connection," I ask, "between
Raj's schemes for productivizing the Negev
and the Arab problem?"

"A close one," says Peres. "We in Israel,
you see, are handicapped not by the shortage
of resources, but by the shortage of peace. If
the Arabs see that we are investing our efforts
in Negev kibbutzim rather than West Bank
settlements, it will introduce a whole new
concept.

"It will indicate that we have turned away
from confrontation towards development.
Our mission is not to master hostile popula-

cc-j

145

tions, but to create and share with our neighbours the benefits of the new technologies. This modern philosophy will unite Israelis and mobilize the country. I believe it."

"The link you mention seems vital: the dialectic between development and peace."

"Yes. Except that we have a third element which makes it complicated, and that is prestige. The Arabs would not like to have anybody think they made concessions in order to secure economic benefits. They do not like associating economic development with politics, they prefer to keep the two apart."

"What do you mean when you say Arabs?" I wanted him to be precise. "The Jordanians, the Egyptians?"

"Yes, both."

"What about the Palestinians?"

"The Palestinians also, though not necessarily the PLO. We have to be careful, though, in making pronouncements. We will be able to speak out one day, when things change on the ground. For the present we should refrain from talking too much about things like the link between economic development and a political settlement. In our hearts however that's the hope. That is even the map.

## Lack of vision, not of talent

"At the risk of sounding either cynical or philosophical," Peres concludes, "I want to say that I think the world is more short of challenges than of brains.

"If brains don't have a challenge and cannot develop opportunities, they are wasted; they disappear from the scene. For that reason I think that politicians should create challenges. If they do the brains will follow. I never saw a serious shortage of brains, but I do see a serious shortage of challenges.

"I want to tell you about two atomic centres: the small one in Nevei-Rubin and the larger one in Dimona. I had a hand in setting them up. The whole scientific community said I was crazy, because at that time it was thought that a small country like Israel could not possibly build an atomic reactor. Now everybody thinks differently, but back in the middle 1950's nuclear energy was thought to be for the super-powers.

"Almost the whole academic profession boycotted my effort, only few wanted to take part in it. They all criticized me. So we went to the Technion. We took young students without experience, without any specialized knowledge of nuclear technology. They learned on the job, they became the generation that built these installations. I would say the challenge to build a nuclear reactor created a generation of nuclear engineers, rather than the other way round. What I have described is only one example.

"Again I say: never a shortage of experts, always a shortage of vision, of daring. The poverty is intellectual, not technological. That is my experience and belief."

"We have also to understand that while maybe the questions don't change, the answers do—every year or two. If we do not stay ahead, we shall begin to lag behind. Ben-Gurion said: 'In defence it is not enough to master present knowledge, you have to foresee what is going to happen tomorrow. If you are merely up-to-date, you are already obsolete.'

"The need is to keep analysing where the world is moving, in which direction it is going. What the future offers to the young generation is tremendous, physically as well as mentally: length of life, richness of life, opportunities in life. But achieving all this requires the ability to innovate; nor is there any need to fear innovation.

"If I may wind up with a Jewish joke: before her wedding a bride bursts into tears.

Her mother asks, why are you crying? She says: I am going to marry an entire stranger. The mother replies: but I did likewise. The girl protests: what are you talking about? You married my father!"

"The young generation think their parents were always married. They do not realize that every generation begins anew."

One of the dangers is precisely that older people feel it is not for them. At Ben-Gurion university, the School of Continuing Education runs a 10-week course for adults. They come to study after a full day's work, and it costs them $2 an hour. To take this on after working hours, and pay for it too shows a high level of motivation. I say to Peres: "They are older people and they want to learn. Their instinct is to remain in touch with the young."

He believes in the principle of dedication. Palestine was in the last century a country so poor, drab and bare that despite its holy associations no outsiders thought it worth settling in on a large scale or colonizing—until Jewish pioneers came and built it up from scratch. These pioneers were idealists with fire in their bellies.

Peres wants more of the same breed for the present revolution, the one that will turn

149

Israel into a high-tech society. "We need selected people who will busy themselves in this new dimension, and not as a one-time effort or a one-time spurt of brilliance.

"They must be endowed with the stamina of a locomotive that has to haul a long train a long way, without deviating from the main track. I have seen this time and again. Whenever we find somebody who believes, who is caught by an idea and devotes his energies and leadership to it, we are in business.

"Raj Reddy's plan for the kibbutzim—and eventually for all the country—requires in the first place a group of enthusiasts whose imagination catches fire. If we find three or four persons in the kibbutz movement ready to take this mission upon themselves, nothing will stop them. The job will get off to an excellent start."

# 9

# "But sir, that's his name!"

Ten years ago in Paris I went to hear a piano recital by a known Palestinian artist. I was intrigued by his talent. Later (when we met) I was impressed by the sober conversation—in faultless French—of this young man, born in Jerusalem during the year when I shed my world war uniform.

Since this first encounter, Ibrahim Souss was appointed by the Palestine Liberation Organization to head its Paris office. It was an interesting choice. He never ceased to hold Parisians under his charm, even in the most difficult moments when terrorist activities, committed and acknowledged by the PLO, generated horror. Souss carried out his role of Palestinian emissary with the same care and precision that he displayed on the piano.

He dominates today's headlines in Jerusalem thanks to a major interview in the *Jerusalem Post*. Following on the uprising by young Palestinians the thunder of violence had to be translated into words.

The words uttered by Ibrahim Souss were published by the Israeli daily. It gave space in its columns to this spokesman of the PLO, Israel's enemy. I was impressed by the editor's professional probity. Did any equivalent French newspaper find space for the words of Ahmed Ben-Bella during the eight long years of the Algerian war? Did the normally exemplary American press open its columns at any time between 1962 and 1973 to Pham-Van-Dong of Vietnam? Nobody wanted to hear the other side. President Johnson put it in a nutshell when he said: "We shall bomb North Vietnam back to the Stone Age."

The question to Souss: "Are you prepared to recognize Israel and talk with the Israelis?"

"Hear me out. In order to understand the deeper feelings of the Israelis and begin to envisage a common life with them, I visited the 'death-camps' of the Nazi Holocaust. I had already been in Dachau and went there again last summer. I am deeply convinced that the Jewish Holocaust belongs to the common heritage of all mankind.

"You know that since the slogan 'Jews to the sea' was first coined by Ahmed Shukeiry

some thirty years ago the PLO has become
more realistic. How can I deny the reality of
the people of Israel? Though no longer
espousing the militant Marxist views of my
youth, I have learned that subjective feelings
cannot change objective reality.

"Ready to talk with the Israelis? The other
day in Paris I was invited to take part in a
public symposium organized by the French
Institute of International Relations. Also
invited was a distinguished Israeli personality
who was passing through the city. I was
confident that he and I would find an opportunity after the debate to have a talk. We were
the same age and had the same kind of education. We were born on the same earth, we
probably had a common future. But it did not
happen."

"You still refuse to recognize Israel."

"Just as Israel does not recognize us. But we
know that when a Palestinian state is created
it will help Israel to tolerate a Palestinian
minority within its borders, just as we shall be
proud to see in our land a flourishing Israeli
minority, which already exists there and
which no-one intends to chase away. Listen,
we shall soon be neighbours, similar to the
French and the Belgians."

Shimon Peres remains distrustful. While welcoming Souss's liberal-minded opinions, he believes the PLO's official policy is very different. The maverick terrorist organization speaks with many voices.

\*　　　\*　　　\*

I leave the front-line of violence and the internal war, now a daily occurrence with its killings, retributions and curfews; not to mention the deafening sounds of world TV presenting pictures, talks and debates. Too many days have elapsed since I was occupied with another task, that of my mission to the universities of this country and this region.

The time for doubts and hesitations is past. We know that the hostilities undermine everything, poison daily life, threaten the very sources of progress. All that is one more reason to try harder. Slowing down would mean certain defeat. Such defeat would be for life, not only in Israel which vacillates under powerful criticism from the entire world, but also in the whole Middle East, where Israel's successful progress so far represents the region's best change for the future.

On Haifa's outskirts in the north I enter the

*"But sir, that's his name!"*

first and most famous of Israel's scientific institutions: the Technion. Here I find the familiar openness of mind, the frank and even striking modesty of Israel's researchers and teachers. They hate propaganda, they have no interest in bragging—all they want is to do their job in peace and quiet.

The weaknesses of the system, hidden by the Technion's world repute, are what they desire to talk about. They are distressed by successive budgetary cuts in favour of military priorities, as is happening in all spheres of civilian research.

The only Technion department where I expected to find no shortage of equipment was Aeronautics. It is the only such faculty in the country, and helps ensure the striking power of Israel's aviation, the ultimate protective shield.

The head of Aeronautics speaks about his immediate concerns. During more than a year he has been demanding four work-stations for his scientists, and he was given none. "I stopped asking," he says, "as no-one even answers me."

What are we talking about? The current price of a work-station of the latest model for universities—in Israel and the US alike—is

155

between $20,000 and $50,000. He was not allocated even one.

But he passes on and speaks to me at his own initiative of the political crisis, the Palestinian resistance, the official Israeli reaction and his own feelings.

"You know," he says, "when I look at what is happening between Jews and Arabs, I always come back to a moment I shall never forget.

"My son underwent open-heart surgery. For four hours I waited anxiously. The first person to come out of the operating-theatre was an Arab doctor, assistant to the main surgeon during the operation. He had good news for me and his face lit up with pleasure: the operation had been successful. We embraced.

"This tells you how I feel towards the Arabs. When we work together the spirit of brotherhood emerges. We are now in a difficult transition period but, looking to the future, I shall always remember how this man, who with his skill and expertise helped save my son, came to me as a friend."

Shimon Peres had heard the complaints of the scientist and the hopes of the father. He acknowledges both, and has something of his own to add.

"Let me tell you a story about another doctor and another occasion," he says. "My son-in-law is a surgeon working at the Tel Ha'Shomer hospital. The other day some young people were brought in from Gaza, who were unfortunately wounded in the riots which took place. A boy aged 14–15 was hit by a bullet and his life was in danger. My son-in-law operated on him. Speaking to the young patient back in the ward he asked: 'What is your name?' The lad replied: 'Jihad.' That means holy war.

"All were aghast. Here is a boy who almost died and yet after the operation, full of pain, he utters a word which is, as you know, a symbol of rebellion. On his card was written Mohammed Geni, no mention of Jihad. Many of the nurses and doctors were taken aback by this extremism.

"The Israeli surgeon went out to speak with the boy's father who, it turned out, was himself a medical practitioner. The man was overjoyed to learn that his boy was fit and well. The Israeli said: 'Your son has radical views. After an operation that saved his life he answered a question about his name by saying "Jihad".' The father burst into laughter. 'That happens,' he said, 'to be his nickname.'

"If I may return to your example, one of the activities which I thought for a long time would really make people come closer to each other is health services. Israeli medicine has made a name for itself, it has become almost a legend. I thought, why not open the doors of medical care to everybody who wants to come?

"I remember visiting one of our army generals at that same Tel Ha'Shomer. He was lying in a ward, right next door to an Arab terrorist who had been caught a few days earlier on the Jordan river. They were under the same roof. I thought that was right.

"We are now building a children's hospital which will probably rank among the most advanced in the world. It will be near the Beilinson hospital in Petah-Tikva. We have made it known already that every child, no matter where he comes from, will qualify for admittance, with no need for passport or visa.

"I go further. When we were disputing over the Taba border enclave, I suggested to the Egyptians that we build and jointly manage an international hospital there. We would bring in the best of our doctors and let whoever is sick come to this place, making it internationally open to everybody. Let us, I said, create a hospital where people are treated in accordance with their pain and not their nationality.

"Unfortunately the idea was rejected by the Egyptians, and I regret it very much. They want first of all to have sovereignty over Taba. I think their refusal was a mistake. I hope a time will come when we shall be able to return to this idea, because I think here is exactly one of those occasions where even if political squabbles are not settled, an avenue can still be found pointing to a better era.

"When I was defence minister I visited our northern frontier and saw refugees from the Lebanese civil war wandering on the other side of the fence. I asked them why they were there. They told me they had fled from their home towns and were adrift. They had no medical treatment, no schools. On the spot we opened two or three stations for medical care. Thousands of people came without crossing any border: the facility was on the border itself. Being influenced by the Chinese I gave it a Chinese-sounding name, 'The Good Fence'.

"I mention this just to show how out of suffering you can seize an opportunity. That applies in other matters."

Everything depends on attitudes. People can be friendly—and just as easily hostile. Politics makes them hostile, but human contact softens asperities. Repeatedly I came across a desire in Israel to express goodwill. Scientists I spoke to in the Technion went as far as to voice a preference for research in two subjects, food and health.

The reason they gave was that these subjects are directly concerned with improving the human lot. "We want to show that the new computer technologies are not just about machines, they are also about living persons."

I talk with Peres about the peace process, but on the political plane. He says: "There are, I think, opportunities for reaching an understanding. I feel that Israel is strong enough to negotiate a peace. Peace will not weaken Israel, it will strengthen her further. We are talking about something that does not just have a price, it brings important benefits. Let me put it this way: peace-making isn't a one-sided act, we don't have to appease each other. Both signatories get mutual and equal advantages.

"The country has to realize that we face three alternatives. The first alternative is the present situation, the status quo. The second is a return to war. That ordeal everyone remembers.

"The third alternative is to build peace, which is something more elusive. Nobody knows what it is and nobody remembers when it last happened. So we suggest here to the thinking person an imagined peace. He must imagine what peace would mean to the Arabs, to the Israelis, to the individual person, to the national interest and, as Jean Monnet said, to the common interest, created in partnership.

"It has always struck me that when you want to study not war but peace, you don't find any books on the subject. All available libraries are libraries on confrontation and hostilities. You can hardly find a library on how to make peace. I don't speak of peace in prophetic terms like the vision of Isaiah; what we are looking for is simply a termination of hostilities between warring neighbours.

"Even that is a complicated process. Particularly in a world which is changing so fast, where peace is a participation in a tremendous race of science, technology and change. It is an invitation to a race, not to a retirement pension.

cc-k

161

"A country with guts can come to terms with its bitterest enemy. Even a little country. I read your comparison in the press between Taiwan and China. It is impressive that a small island originally barren of resources stands up to a giant and hostile nation on the mainland with over one billion inhabitants. How did it overcome this disparity in power? By taking the subject of scientific and economic development seriously. Taiwan did so well that it now enjoys the second biggest foreign trade surplus in the world after Japan.

"Result? This offshore island is carefully studied, as a model development, by Communist China with science and investments. Such an outcome was unimaginable forty years ago: it is the reality of today.

"One of the problems, you see," Peres goes on, "is the misgivings which surround the message of peace. Is the other side—people ask—willing to make a settlement?

"Although they see the hurled stone as immediate, as real, as tangible, they cannot see the olive branch in the same category. The danger is manifest, it is round the corner. You see it on television. Peace is insubstantial. When the subject is raised the Arab world turns very timid. Some of our friends among them say they dare not talk about their willingness for peace because it puts them in an embarrassing situation. Unbelievable, but true."

"Still when you, Shimon Peres, see this new generation of Palestinians in an uprising, with a passion to take control of their own future—something normal in every population—and you see the State of Israel keeping law and order by sending young striplings of the same age as the Palestinians to this street fight, to this raging war—you must have some feeling of what is in the hearts of both sides."

*That automatic reflex again: Peres reverts to his mistrust.* I press him to explain. He does: "The thing with the Palestinians that makes everything so difficult is their lack of representation. They were never able to organize themselves into an orderly political force. It is like a strategy without a policy, it runs wild.

"Their leadership is an emigrant leadership, located for the last twenty years outside the country. We know that its control is symbolic, not real. Not only that: the PLO is divided. If there are moderate elements under this roof of organization they are indecisive, incapable of exploiting opportunities. When I watch them I feel they are following the headlines in the papers and not the real events among their own people. They don't share the sufferings of the Palestinians, they live outside the country. What kind of leadership is that?"

"But you have Palestinians who live here. When you go into the cities of the West Bank you find responsible people among them. There is surely a method by which they could choose their delegates. There must be a way for the Palestinians to be represented, if that is what you are looking for in the quest for peace."

He takes me up on that, he wants me to understand the obstacles. "You are raising a crucial question," he admits. "Yes, we have to speak to the Palestinians, but also with the Jordanians, you mustn't forget them. You mention representation. In some Arab countries life is not based on that, it is based on control. Power lies with whoever has the army, whoever has the money, whoever has the cruelty to rule.

"We conclude that we have to deal not only with the people who do the representing, but also at times with those who have the power of decision. Declarations in a vacuum are not enough, not even grandiose ones.

"As defence minister I proposed free elections for mayors in the West Bank. It was very controversial in the Cabinet. Ministers warned that in a free vote PLO people would be elected and we should be turning over the West Bank to the terrorists. In spite of that I insisted that the elections be held. I think it was the only free and real ballot that ever took place in an Arab community. Nobody will contradict that. I made the rounds in many towns and villages on election day, without policemen, without soldiers. I went to the polling stations. Incidentally we gave the right of vote to women.

"Once the results were out my critics alleged triumphantly that most of the elected candidates were indeed PLO. But I knew them and they were not PLO. They used the language of PLO, otherwise they would not have been elected. Though honest and fair-minded people, they had to make extremist declarations.

"After the elections I was supposed to appear on TV with one of them, who agreed to participate. A couple of hours before the deadline he called me and said, 'Forgive me, Mr. Peres, but if I appear with you I shall have to pay a very heavy price. You know my feelings, you know where I stand, but I cannot take part.' I understood him.

"When I went to negotiate with the newly-elected Palestinian representatives they had only one thing to say: 'Go and speak with the PLO'. You see, they are prisoners, they cannot function by themselves. They need backing, from the PLO.

"To this very day no Arab leader, other than Sadat, has been ready to take the leap, to take on the job of being realistic and not demagogic. That is the greatest tragedy that I see—for them and for us. I appreciate their feelings, their need to have everything their own way. But they must also take our attitude into account. Our security problems are not a joke, they must be treated seriously.

"We have to compromise, we have to find a middle ground on which to meet; otherwise it is a nonsense. To sum up: the situation is that they are not strong enough to overpower us, and not wise enough to meet us half way."

*"You said you wanted to speak about the first step towards the peace process."*

"Many people think that in order to make

peace you must refrain from revealing what
will be your ultimate concession until the final
stage in the talks. There is some truth in that;
but what we have to think about is not the
final stage. The most difficult part of the
negotiating process is the opening of it. I think
we have to concentrate on the first step. Let us
analyse this first step.

"For many years the Jordanians said: 'We
are ready to negotiate with Israel provided the
Americans and the Israelis, or at least one of
the two, tell us before the negotiations what
will be the outcome. Otherwise what is the
point of starting talks?

"We have worked hard to explain that this
approach is impossible. An Israeli who
announces ahead of time what will be the
result of the negotiations is out of business.
That is not how it works. Our counter-offer
is: let us negotiate without prior conditions.

"They answer: 'Look, if we tell our people
that we are going to negotiate without prior
guarantees, we risk our lives.' There you have
it, this is what has been our constant dilemma.

"We reached the following conclusion: that
if we want to negotiate without prior conditions we have to find a way of doing it.
According to the Arabs the best safeguard

would be an international opening, an international conference.

"Summoning a conference is not enough, we have to know what kind of conference it will be. The first necessity is to fix its powers and prerogatives; who will attend is a secondary matter.

"I consider it a great achievement that we have reached an understanding with the Americans. They agree that the convening governments will have to give up three privileges: (a) The privilege to impose a solution; that must be waived; (b) The privilege to negotiate instead of leaving the negotiating to the disputing parties. The talks will be direct. (c) The privilege to undo any bilateral agreement to which Israel is a party; that must be waived as well.

"The minute these three conditions are met, Russian participation ceases to be dangerous. On the contrary if the Soviets normalize their diplomatic relations with Israel before the conference, which Gorbachev now states is a possibility; and if they change their policy towards Soviet Jews—then I believe their presence at the conference-table will be actually beneficial.

"We now have a strange situation. The

*"But sir, that's his name!"*

Jordanians are for an international conference (of some sort). The Egyptians are for it. The Americans are in favour. But Israel remains half and half."

# 10

## Pessimists are more serious

The rivalry since World War Two between the major opposing ideologies—Washington and Moscow—has dominated the world and channelled people's savings into arms expenditure. Governments fell hostage to weapon manufacturers, who managed constantly to expand their connections and increase their power.

Having more guns and planes than the other side became the touchstone for national survival. Those who manufactured engines of destruction were acclaimed, they were seen as patriots serving the national cause. Their critics who opposed militarism were dismissed contemptuously as 'peacemongers'.

The most profitable type of hostility for the arms dealers is not the barrel that bursts into a single destructive conflagration, but the feud that remain continuously on red-hot embers, generating clashes and losses without ever flaming up into a final Armageddon.

Such is the Middle East.

The world's most long-standing conflict seems the most ineradicable. Five wars in 40 years—and the same foes readying themselves for the next encounter, with three times the arms they had at the last cease-fire. How to restore peace in this region of hate and violence?

"Nowhere has war been tested so often over the centuries as in the Middle East," Shimon Peres reflects this evening. "And each time the only result was a worsening of the human condition."

All the world is focussed on Israel. The flow of news, messages, calls and visitors never ceases. His mind remains glued to the peace process. Everything is at a standstill in Jerusalem, in Washington, among the Arabs. Where to begin?

"Suppose," says Peres, "we don't find peace with the Arabs, can anyone after all these decades of conflict say: 'Let's return to the panacea of war?' We have made at least one discovery over the years, that war solves nothing.

"It has to be prevented. That cannot be achieved by doing nothing, by waiting. Political wisdom requires being ahead of the storm.

Hesitating until it is over can be fatal. Five minutes before the storm can save the situation; five minutes after may be too late.

"We are now in the middle of the storm. The present convulsion does not distinguish between Israelis, Palestinians, Americans, Russians—it affects all participants. The need to stop is common to all."

❊     ❊     ❊

Peace cannot be imposed, it must be given shape in a dialogue between the combatants. Up to now they refuse to talk or even extend mutual recognition. Hence the need for an international conclave as the way to get things moving. After a start is made the two sides will have to face up to the problem and reach an understanding.

Up till now progress seemed impossible because the Jews and Arabs not only fight, they cannot tolerate each other. Officially they do not acknowledge each other's existence. Hostile governments still look upon the State of Israel as the "Zionist entity". They see Jewish statehood as a historic aberration.

Israel for its part only talks on a government-to-government basis, whether over

173

matters of war or peace, and finds it hard to discuss with an organization that functions by terrorist methods, therefore dismissed as non-legitimate.

Israel has two ways of reacting to this impasse. One is to declare a fight to the finish against the insurrectionists. The other is to show a different kind of courage, to defy threats and insults and meet up with the enemy round a bargaining table. Those who choose this course must be ready to settle on a compromise that will satisfy no-one, but will stop the killing and let young people get on at last with their lives.

Is Shimon Peres ready for such a down-to-earth encounter?

"We are ready and willing to meet with Palestinians, but authentic Palestinian representatives, those who can decide to do something positive, not just to kill.

"The King of Morocco once remarked that 'the whole Middle East has experienced only war, you won't find a single nation there familiar with peace'. That is an observation worth remembering.

"Europe is more fortunate," Peres continues, "it had the experience of both war and peace. The United States has hardly any

174

experience of war on its own territory. But the Middle East is at present entirely locked in war. People would like to reduce these tensions but don't know how.

"They cannot see that peace is not just lack of war. It is much more, it is a new dimension, a fresh opening. It is not merely getting rid of something troublesome, it is creating an exciting new situation.

"Men fear to think about peace. It introduces big changes, upsets old habits, harms vested interests. That is why it does not look as attractive as it should. It requires firm decisions; instead all we see is nervousness and uncertainty.

"Over a long period of recorded history there were in the Middle East more than thirty changes of guard, changes of domination. Every 200 years on the average another power took over.

"We now come to the Palestinian people: their position is the worst of all. They have never in their history enjoyed one day of independence, one day of peace, one day of freedom. So they cannot see the wider horizons and opportunities.

"We encounter also a problem deep-rooted in human psychology. Throughout the region people who are pessimists by nature are taken more seriously than those who are optimists.

"I decided at a certain point in my life to become an imperfect optimist rather than a perfect pessimist.

"Optimism is treated with great reservations in the Middle East, even with worry. Anybody delivering an optimistic message is considered naive, he is dismissed as unrealistic. This is one of the psychological barriers we have to overcome."

"I find it attractive that you should be, as you say, a decided optimist."

"I said: an imperfect optimist."

My feeling over the last few months is that Shimon Peres believes increasingly in the possibility of a settlement. How can the necessary initiative be taken and things moved in a new direction? Two historic precedents merit consideration.

*          *          *

The armistice talks of Pan-Mun-Jongh, held between the two sides in the Korean war (one side supported by America, the other by China and the Soviet Union) were protracted for years without reaching any conclusion.

When campaigning for the presidency

General Eisenhower suddenly came out with a simple statement that turned out to be momentous: "I shall go to Korea."

The shock was electric. When voted into the White House he carried out his promise and betook himself on the long journey to the distant negotiating-table, where the parties were stuck in procedural tangles. His presence on the spot and his desire to bring things to a head spurred the adversaries to shake off their lethargy and make a response.

Issues that appeared insoluble—demarcation lines, the division of the country, the time-table for withdrawal, guarantees for the future—found a decision within weeks. Hostilities were terminated; the blood-letting ceased and was never resumed. The only dispute currently troubling the relations of North and South Korea concerns the location of the coming Olympic Games.

You may of course argue that it is not the same thing. Here in the Middle East there is a mass of complicating factors. There two armies, two regimes, two super-powers, faced each other, and the rules of the game were clear. It sounds straightforward, but in fact the circumstances were not quite so propitious at the time.

cc-l

It is easy to talk lightly about the Korean episode now it is all over; 30 years ago things were far from simple. A country had to be deliberately split in two by mutual agreement in the heat of a quarrel. An arbitrary border had to be drawn up fixing permanent limits. It was a tough assignment, yet preferable to continued war; and the contract was honoured.

\*       \*       \*

The story of the war and the eventual peace in Indochina is most instructive. This dependency was France's most ancient and rich overseas possession. From the north in Hanoi to the south in Saigon it was prosperous and unassailable. The Japanese had been driven out. Now the French army, backed by a powerful Pacific fleet, assured the integrity of the territory. The Indochinese were granted autonomy under Emperor Bao-Dai, who negotiated a treaty of association with the government in Paris.

Nobody took any notice of the acts of violence perpetrated here and there by communist terrorists, instigated from afar by a mythical agitator called Ho-Chi-Minh. He seemed powerless, a symbolic figure without an army. He would easily, it was thought, be isolated from his supporters. Overlooked was his mystical radicalism, which made him impervious to the facts. He could ignore that the odds were against him, he took no account of the crushing superiority of the French in firepower.

Eight years later France found itself on the defensive, facing a highly-organized and nationalistic population headed by that same Ho-Chi-Minh. The growing peril to the French administration, combined with some anxiety among the super-powers about international repercussions, brought the participants in what had come to be the Indochinese war to a conference in Geneva.

French ministers Bidault and Pleven (foreign affairs and defence respectively) agreed to negotiate with representatives of Russia and China. They took little notice of a Vietnamese "terrorist" whom the two powers had brought in their trail, Pham-Van-Dong, head of the resistance's "provisional government", the Vietminh.

One French parliamentarian only, Pierre Mendes-France, spoke up. He made an impassioned speech in the National Assembly on this subject each year for seven successive years. He showed that the conflict in Indochina had cost France since 1948 a sum equal to all the funds received from Washington under the Marshall Plan.

The "dirty war" in the French colony sacrificed each year the equivalent of an entire graduating class at the military officers' school of St. Cyr—this apart from the setback to the economic upbuilding of the country caused by the government's incapacity to put an end to a military engagement which had no issue.

Mendes-France was a lone voice because what he said was true and the truth had to be hidden for as long as possible, in the hope of a miracle. His demand for negotiations met always with the same argument, that "there was nobody to negotiate with".

There were only terrorists, and their own ranks were divided between Communists and Buddhists, between splinter-groups linked to China and splinter-groups linked to the Soviet Union. The coalition between these elements was good for killing and destroying, not for constructive talks. The existence itself of Ho-Chi-Minh was disputed. He was, it was said, no more than a face on a picture postcard.

Despite this reluctance to come to grips

with the essential problem (the rise of nationalism) France consented to a parley at Geneva in 1953. Attending were the permanent members of the Security Council: the US, the Soviet Union, China, France and Britain; the various Indochinese governments: Vietnam, Laos and Cambodia; and representatives of the several resistance movements, one of them the Vietminh.

The conference had a single purpose, to offer a legitimate framework for dialogue between the disputing parties. But the French government could not come to terms with this necessity. It thought up devices to gain time, it tried all means to avoid direct talks with the enemy.

On 17 June 1954, after an unforeseen and crushing setback at Dien-Bien-Phu, the politicians were finally at a loss. To expose the proposals of Mendes-France as an impractical dream they submitted his name to Parliament for the premiership, confident he would be rejected.

On the podium he stated bluntly: "We could have bargained for a better peace before, when we had more trumps in our hands. But it is not too late. An armistice must be concluded. The government that I shall form will

181

set itself a time limit of four weeks. If within that period no pact is achieved I shall leave office. My aim is peace."

Voted (despite all predictions to the contrary) as head of the government, Mendes-France made his way to Geneva where he initiated direct contact with ... the neglected head of the Vietminh delegation, Pham-Van-Dong. The other powers were kept informed: the US and Britain on one side, the USSR and China on the other. Agreement was reached in broad lines. The French prime minister conceded North Vietnam to the Vietminh nationalist movement, and a frontier was fixed along the 17th parallel. The southern area would go to the pro-French population, and would be evacuated by the Vietminh maquis. On these terms the outline of a pact was drafted.

The powers dragged their feet: Pham-Van-Dong argued for hours with the Russians and the Chinese every night to no avail. Each delegation wanted extra concessions from the French, sure that Mendes-France would sell out anything in order to return with a treaty in his pocket.

I was at Mendes-France's side as his junior aide. We felt that the delegates considered the "four-week ultimatum" a bluff. As we strolled round the lake on the eve of his scheduled last day, I suggested that two official aircraft be summoned from Paris at dawn to load the baggage. Mendes-France made it known that he was going back to France that evening as planned.

Molotov and Chou-En-Lai remained sceptical, but Pham-Van-Dong would not let them take the risk. His people were the victims of the fighting, he did not want to miss the chance presented.

At 5 o'clock that afternoon we received a phone call at Mendes-France's villa. The three plenipotentiaries in the other villa across the city requested a get-together in an hour's time. Mendes-France instructed the pilots to warm up the engines, audibly. Then he went over to the meeting. It lasted all night. At dawn peace was signed.

France was relieved of a burden which had bled its youth and mortgaged its resources. The Vietminh nationalists won their portion of land, on which to build their future.

*   *   *

If Indochina fell later into a still more savage war that was because France, drawn into another conflict in Algeria, found it necessary to call in the American army to relieve its forces in Vietnam. The tragic consequences of this historic mistake—for Vietnam, for America and for the world—are known.

But they should not conceal from us today the fact that bilateral negotiations between the two sides locked in battle had ended in a successful compact of understanding.

The eventual closure of the two wars (in South-East Asia and North Africa) made possible in due course an advance in France towards new objectives, with the accent on youth, development and the future. In the Middle East today peace would also open the door to a fresh era of progress and prosperity for all.

※          ※          ※

"We have formed a concept that I would call the greening of the Middle East," said Shimon Peres. "Maybe it should be organized initially not by foreign ministers but by ministers of agriculture. Let us have all the agricultural ministers of the Middle East meet and deal with the basic issues of both our lives and theirs, which are: overcoming aridity; introducing irrigation systems; tapping energy sources; applying new technologies to the cultivation of the land; keeping the sea free from pollution, so as to maintain reserves of fish life and for other reasons.

"Scientific proposals for improving farming in our region under conditions of peace ought to arouse considerable interest. Furthermore the need is greater in the Arab countries than in Israel, because of their rate of birth. Egypt, Iran and Turkey will contain, each of them, 100m. people by the first quarter of the next century. Where will their food come from?

"Every Arab country is going to double its population in the coming 25 years. You cannot feed children with guns and shells and missiles, you have to provide vegetables and fruit, clothes and shelter. This brings us back to the Mediterranean. Don't take a political bird's eye view, but a scientific bird's eye view. What to do with this lake and all the inhabitants around it; how to organize it, not politically but scientifically? Politics are not enough, there must be a scientific answer to the needs of the people.

"You can mobilize the cooperation of Europe, Japan, the industries, the banking institutions, the governments, all of which, I am sure, will gladly participate in the development of the zone to the east of the Mediterranean, instead of assisting in its destruction. They have invested hundreds of billions of dollars in arms and politics, and the result was only to increase hatred. With a fraction of this investment they could give the whole area a positive impetus.

"Unless constructive change happens, the problems will become worse. The situation is never static. If you do not overcome the desert, the desert will overcome you."

\*　　　\*　　　\*

There is little doubt by now that negotiations must start soon. Events move at a breathtaking pace, and individuals are beginning to open their minds to hard realities. Everybody realizes that a resumption of hostilities would be a hopeless confession of impotence.

Negotiations must take place. They will end in a compromise allowing all parties to devote themselves to what is urgent and essential: education, modernization, catching up with the future. What are the factors which are going to dominate these discussions and determine their outcome?

The crucial needs that must be met are two:

—The security of Israel within its frontiers.

—The legitimate aspirations of the Palestinians.

These questions have been on the table for continuous decades, and remain without an answer. Here are three possible options:

First option: territorial partition.

Inhabitants of the territories get sovereignty over a part of Palestine. They receive what they most need, a land of their own, ruled neither by Israel nor Jordan. The Palestinian people would acquire at last their own nationhood.

An important problem is left pending: the new regime would be unstable, therefore erratic and reckless. It might mobilize an army at the very gates of Jerusalem, aided and supplied by the Soviet Union. Such a setup is not acceptable to the Israelis.

If this Gordian knot cannot be unravelled in the negotiations, other alternatives must be sought.

Second option: autonomy.

The Palestinian people enjoy self-government in their own territory, with their own identity, flag and parliament, subject—as concerns their internal affairs—to no-one. Two domains remain under Israeli control: foreign affairs and defence.

This autonomy solution, incorporated in the Camp David agreement, is supported and promoted by the United States. It is not acceptable to the Palestinians. It is favoured by the right wing in Israel, but with reservations. Opponents point to recent historical precedents indicating that autonomy invariably leads to independence and sovereignty.

The first option is not agreeable to the Israelis, the second not to the Palestinians. Is there a third possibility, offering better perspectives?

Third option: confederation.

A new concept has come up in discussion that merits examination by both sides. It provides all the necessary safeguards, without modifying the right of the Palestinians to self-rule.

The idea is to form a "community", on the model of the European Economic Community, between Jordan, Palestine and Israel. Each member-state is an equal partner, with its own parliament, government and national identity. Each is at the same time part of the greater whole, which ensures strategic security as well as fostering economic prosperity for all.

Such a confederation, if it can be achieved, would become the kernel of a larger commonwealth, embracing in the course of time the whole of the Middle East, providing a common market in goods, manpower, capital and development. A treaty of association between Israel, Jordan and Palestine would break with chauvinist traditions. It would be an act of trust, an expression of the will to live and create.

This third option, though seemingly visionary, deserves inclusion all the same, so that no possibility of ending the lengthy stalemate is overlooked in the months ahead.

# 11

# The choice

The route south is not long, from the ramparts of Jerusalem to the bare brown hills of the Negev. In less than an hour we reach the capital of the desert, Beersheba; and it is another world.

Here lies the future of Israel. Here live the pioneers with the fruits of their labour. Around the largest "desert university" to be found anywhere, enterprising research institutes prepare the transformation of arid areas. The Study Centre for Desert Research and the Desert Agronomy Centre work out on their computers the optimal utilization of humidity and sunshine.

They keep under observation huge conservatories, whose fruit, trees and vegetables measure up to and often outstrip in quality and variety other countries' produce on world markets. There is also the Water Desalination Institute. It endeavours to sweeten saline and brackish waters, the non-potable fluid that covers half the globe, just as rainless desert covers half its land portion.

Here means of life are extracted from sources that are themselves lifeless. Man is creating a second planet, another earth. Each step out of Beersheba is a pilgrimage, a renewal; you are surrounded by a pure simplicity that is primeval. Here no man has killed as yet or stolen or conquered. Each bud that grows, each drop of fresh moisture is the fruit of human intelligence.

The beauty of the great golden plains of the Negev is framed by handsome mountain ranges. They guide your vision in three strategic directions: towards the Red Sea, the Jordan kingdom and Egypt. All three locations border on and delimit the great Israeli oasis, which possesses a quality that softens and appeases. The struggle for life, the bloody contest for survival, seems in suspense. It may be possible here, and later everywhere, to create life without tearing it away from others.

Beersheba was a small shepherds' village when Israel's great shepherd, David Ben-Gurion, found there the embodiment of his dreams and decided to build a model on the spot for others to emulate. Today Ben-Gurion University of the Negev, which has become the heart of Beersheba, spreads its departments, laboratories and residential areas over hitherto untrodden territories. Around it, as in California, a city has grown of 125,000 inhabitants.

The second generation of Negev pioneers, now adult and creative, graduates of Ben-Gurion University, have already left the throngs and noise of this young city to beget a series of small satellite townships within fifty kilometres of the regional capital. The peopling of the desert may well turn the Negev into Israel's focal point by the end of the century.

David Ben-Gurion set an example by reaching beyond Beersheba and settling in a kibbutz further south: Sde Boker.

There can be no more aesthetic abode. Nothing in his house has been touched since his death. The four rooms in which he lived and worked are left as they were: two private rooms, his and his wife's; a lounge and a dining-room, panelled with bookshelves; a veranda. Around that, up to the horizon, the luminosity of the desert.

His private room to the left of the front door contains a bed and a work-table. In it he took refuge, read and wrote. On the walls nothing—save a single large framed

CC-M

picture: that of Gandhi.

How remarkable that of all the sages and prophets who inspired Ben-Gurion he should have chosen one visage to stay throughout the day in the intimacy of his room, remaining there after his death almost as a testament: the visage of Mahatma Gandhi.

The doctrine of non-violence did not seem destined to captivate Israel's war leaders. It was pointed out to me back in Jerusalem that there is also in that room a bust of Socrates. I did not see it, presumably it is secreted somewhere. The solitary glow of Gandhi's lean and dark features, in this picture chosen by Ben-Gurion, dominates the scene.

The armed prophet of the Jewish people, who fought wars to found and defend his country, had wanted (it seems) to bequeath a still greater legacy when placing Gandhi above the place where he sat each day. Ben-Gurion had taken this opportunity of heralding a future without violence, which should allow the creative genius that exists in all men to blossom.

He could not predict when the new order of things would occur. He knew that it must eventuate some time, and that the desert would be its source and fount. Sure enough the fifteen years between his death and the centenary of his birth, recently celebrated, have seen a flowering of the needed sciences, a birth of the "knowledge era" which may change the course of the future.

This scientific millennium was the ideal he had in view. The struggles on the battlefield were only a means to this end. In the privacy of his room he commemorated not the feats of arms associated with his leadership, but the image of a superior being who had no other weapon than moral force, the force of the spirit, the force of example.

Numerous letters were exchanged between the liberator of India and the builder of Israel. They are kept, together with the 500 notebooks of his diary, in his personal archives. The collection is housed at a study centre headed in Sde Boker by Professor Illan Troen.

The young historian received me obligingly three times within a single month at his desert workplace in Sde Boker. He opened the dossiers of Ben-Gurion's correspondence. I wanted to read a particular message sent by Gandhi—in his own hand—on the eve of the battle for Israel's independence.

"My sympathies," writes the Mahatma, "are with the Jews. They have been the untouchables of Christianity. The parallel between their treatment by the Christians and the treatment of the untouchables by the Hindus under the British is very close—most inhuman. Apart from friendship therefore there is a more universal reason for my sympathy for the Jews.

"Certainly the tyrants through the ages never went as mad as Hitler, and the persecution of the Jews seems to have no parallel in history! This is one more reason for the Jews to consider that they can settle in Palestine— not by reducing the proud Arabs (that would be a crime against humanity) but only by converting the Arab heart, and gaining the goodwill of the Arabs originating from the same land.

"The Jews can prove their claim to be the 'chosen race' by choosing non-violence to vindicate their position on earth. A Jewish friend has sent me a book by Cecil Roth. There I can see a whole record of what the Jews have done to enrich the world's literature, art, science, medicine, agriculture. Now they can add to their own unsurpassed contribution the still-surpassing contribution of non-violent action."

Are Ben-Gurion's disciples ready, on the

fortieth anniversary of the state's foundation—which is also the year of the Palestinian
uprising—for a metamorphosis? Ben-Gurion
himself gave a pointer after the Six Day War
by opposing the continued occupation of
Arab territory and urging its evacuation.

Moshe Dayan was reminded as foreign
minister of this stand by the first Arab head of
government personally to recognize Israel,
Anwar Sadat of Egypt. Two interconnected
treaties were finalized at Camp David, one
spelling out the withdrawal from all Egyptian
territories conquered by the Israeli army; the
other offering political autonomy to Arab
Palestine, with free elections, and negotiation
with Israel for the departure of the military.

The first treaty was fulfilled: Sinai has been
evacuated. The agreement on autonomy has
yet to be applied. The question posed twenty
years ago by Ben-Gurion and ten years ago by
Sadat continues to demand an answer. Both
the peace of the region and Israel's destiny are
at stake. The question is no longer what the
Arabs need or do not need. The issue is the
very human adventure called Zionism.

Believers have either to re-discover its true
inspiration and justification, which have
nothing to do with domination by force and

everything to do with a leap forward in the field of knowledge; or else they yield to the sirens, old as mankind, who nurture the military illusion. If they choose the latter course, the message of Zionism will gradually fade from the pages of history.

*It follows that the negotiation is with the Arabs only in appearance. The matter to be decided rests with the Israelis and has to be settled among them.*

They face a new historic enterprise, whose consequences will be as great as the original venture they undertook four decades ago. In essence their predicament is unchanged: to fear or not to fear. Then it was fear of invading Arab armies; today it is fear of sacrificing old values (nationalism) to make way for new ones (education, science, the blossoming of each individual). It is a choice not only between alternative policies but between alternative societies, alternative lives.

Of all the statesmen with whom I have held intellectual converse, the one with whom the dialogue lasted longest and went deepest seems to be this man, born in White Russia, who became a Zionist militant and then a military organizer, and finally a moral leader: Shimon Peres.

## The choice

We never were on intimate personal terms but a particular relationship has grown between us, derived from the sense that we are from the same intellectual workshop. When we meet after long periods of separation, we resume effortlessly the flow of discussion. He knows and loves France; I have always been an admirer of the abilities of the Israelis; we became jointly concerned over the fate of the US; we discovered the economic performance of Japan; we jointly responded to the promises of the computer age.

All these things nourish our exchange. Now I take up with him the question of the portrait in Sde Boker:

"How do you explain Ben-Gurion's fascination with Gandhi? Why this reverence of the warrior for the apostle? Is it not striking that the father of Israel should have put up this particular portrait alone on his wall for posterity to see? I feel there is here a message to unravel."

Preoccupied for so long with the physical defence of his country, Shimon Peres had not given much thought to the symbolism of Ben-Gurion's last unspoken message. He now weighed the matter up. The two leaders, he conceded, had, with all their differences, a lot in common:

"Ben-Gurion was impressed with one of Gandhi's qualities, which he emulated: leadership by example. If you want the people to follow you, you have to demonstrate with your own acts what they should do.

"Gandhi went to his village; Ben-Gurion went to his village. They both gave up comforts. People are terribly suspicious about leaders, thinking they want power in order to have a good time. It is extremely important that leadership should be separated from wealth and the good life. People know their own weakness and expect statesmen to provide an example of moral strength.

"I believe Ben-Gurion and Gandhi shared the same approach: the way they dressed, the way they ate. Gandhi was most of his life clad in a loin-cloth. Ben-Gurion wore shorts and a shirt without a tie, dressed in khaki and lived in a barracks. He paid no attention to food, he considered feasting a waste of time. Simplicity of life, that was one joint quality.

"The second was a tremendous desire to return to the state of genesis and original purity, before nature was spoilt by human cunning. Ben-Gurion wanted a return not to the elements of life but to the elemental life, to the beginning of things where really great matters have their origin. And that again typified the two of them.

"The third thing was that they would never limit themselves to a narrow concept of power. Power is not just physical power. Gandhi thought it is non-violence; that is also a power. Non-violence does not mean no power, it means power of a different kind, one not involving the mailed fist.

"A fourth point is something basic: that no matter how powerful people are, justice is a major consideration. You have to be fair-minded, your conduct must be dominated by moral considerations.

"I think these four qualities are to be found, in a similar way, in Gandhi and Ben-Gurion."

\*　　　　\*　　　　\*

Gandhi back among us, today? It might be relevant, at a time when two important truths have come to the fore.

The first is that all violent actions taken to settle human problems, whether between individuals, societies or nations, contain in themselves the ultimate destruction of the perpetrator. It is the history of all empires, but the lesson has never been learned—till now.

201

# The Chosen and the Choice

Today in 1988 the conclusion applies to the conflict between East and West and is the reason for the successive summits between Moscow and Washington, designed deliberately to reduce their military arsenals. It applies also and for the first time to the still persistent conflict between Jews and Arabs.

Educating me in the trends of thought of this region Shimon Peres lets me have a text from a rabbi known and respected in Israel, David Hartman, entitled "Perspectives of the Israel–Palestine Conflict". I read: "The Palestinian revolt has made us aware as never before that the Palestinians possess a national consciousness.

"Either we recognize their fundamental desire and seek to accommodate it, or we shall create a society that rules with force and intimidation. The latter alternative, if chosen, will inevitably undermine our renaissance. For two-thousand years we never imagined that a restored Jewish nation could possibly suppress and humiliate another people. As long as the Palestinians are homeless victims, we shall feel like strangers in our own land.

"A Palestinian political entity, in which they find themselves responsible for the well-being of their citizens, may begin the process of healing the present destructive urge of many Palestinians. If we continue to control them, then we feed this destructive urge. There is a vicious dialectic that must be broken: in trying to control them, we lose ourselves.

"The Bible does not begin with the history of Abraham or with the liberation struggle of Israel from Egypt—but with the story of God as the Creator of all life. What the act of Creation signifies for the understanding of our spiritual heritage can be seen in the three benedictions recited after meals.

"The first benediction addresses God as the Creator of all life; in the second we thank God for the Covenant and the land; and the third expresses our yearning for the re-building of Jerusalem. The order of these benedictions teaches us that only after we acknowledge our solidarity with all of humanity can we give thanks for our own particular heritage.

"The anger and bitterness of the past must not inhibit new thinking or bold initiatives. A total commitment to resolve the conflict with the Palestinians will be the finest expression of loyalty to our tradition."

The second great truth discovered by the present generation is that the scientific age in its latest form is no longer the exclusive concern of the scientific and managerial sectors. It is the affair for the first time of the commonalty of ordinary people, young and old.

It spells the end of institutionalized hierarchies, of commands from above, of the power of the few over the many. Social slavery will cease both in the supposedly liberal-capitalist societies and the supposedly socialist-collectivist ones. Past ideologies had this in common, that they all locked the individual into a system. The system deprived him of autonomy and thus denied him his role as a creator.

Computer networks place all existent knowledge at the disposal of each person. It is now up to him. Universality of access allows him to use his imagination freely for creative purposes.

Mankind thus finds a foothold in a new continent, *the land of knowledge*. At first that land was like yesterday's Negev, beautiful and bare. Tomorrow it will be like that same Negev when it is in full bloom, an open space for body and soul, a promised land for the human intelligence. Anachronistic adventures—territories, domination, racialism—will lose all meaning. In their place will be two immense challenges, one to open the secrets of space, the other to open the secrets of the human brain.

When gazing at the tulips, superbly coloured, grown artificially in the sunny, computerized greenhouses of the Negev and exported—no less—to the motherland of tulips, Holland, one gets a sense of the change overtaking the world. Like the bread and wine of Jaures these flowers are no longer natural crops sprouting from the soil, they are "a marvellous human artifact".

They are like the present-day processed vines yielding Bordeaux vintages on other continents. The stems went through a phase of scanning, splitting and grafting with the aid of computers over a six-month period by Japanese chemists in the west of France, until they were ready for transplanting to the slopes of Mount Fuji.

The abandonment of parochialism and the substitution of the world view are given expression by the first Japanese Nobel prizewinner in medicine, Susumi Tonegawa. *He explains retrospectively the decision to carry out his higher studies in the US: "I must tell my compatriots two things which concern our future as Japanese people. The instruction I received here in America left a much greater space for the critical spirit than the system we have at home. I would never have won this prize had I remained within the rigid educational framework of my native land.*

*"Second, the English language is superior to ours not only for communication, but as a tool for reasoning. This deserves fresh thinking."*

Thus the world questions accepted norms, dogmas, traditions. Everybody can have access to the best that the universe can supply, to the treasures of knowledge, logic and instruction now becoming available to all.

✻　　　✻　　　✻

I end my working trip in Israel, the third in a year. I ask Shimon Peres what objective he will now pursue. He would like—he answers—to make a start at the practical level: Israel must do three things: make all its industries science-based; give every citizen extensive education; and create an infra-structure of business relations with Asia. Peace will accelerate these developments."

Only yesterday the world was founded on the antagonisms of the superpowers. The cost, the sacrificed resources, the corruption and sterility are bringing this primitive phase to a close. The Western and Soviet empires have discovered that their struggle is choking them, while free minds in Asia have been conquering world markets and are now taking over the centres of action.

In Jerusalem, too, this "elite people, dominant and sure of itself", to use De Gaulle's phrase, has found that it may be losing control of its destiny. A daily reading of the Israeli press in Hebrew and English reveals how far from being "sure of itself" this nation of individualists engaged in a thoroughgoing self-scrutiny is. The next forty years will not be a continuation of the last forty years.

Two forms of patriotism exist side by side. Patriotism of territory and patriotism of indentity. A clear choice must be made—now.

# ANNEXES

1. Partition Plan                           211
2. Declaration of Independence              215
3. Palestine National Convention            219
4. Resolutions 242 and 338                  225
5. Camp David                               227
6. The World Jewish Population              236

CC-N

# PARTITION

The United Nations Special Commission for Palestine (UNSCOP) recommended to the General Assembly of the UN on 3 September 1947 "the partition of Palestine into Arab and Jewish States and an international regime for Jerusalem, all three linked in an Economic Union."
The following are extracts from the commission's report.

1. The Committee held a series of informal discussions during its deliberations in Geneva as a means of appraising comprehensively the numerous aspects of the Palestine problem. In these discussions the members of the Committee debated at length and in great detail the various proposals advanced for its solution.

2. In the early stages of the discussions, it became apparent that there was little support for either of the solutions which would take an extreme position, namely, a single independent State of Palestine, under either Arab or Jewish domination. It was clear, therefore, that there was no disposition in the Committee to support in full the official proposals of either the Arab States or the Jewish Agency as described in Chapter IV of this report. It was recognized by all members that an effort must be made to find a solution which would avoid meeting fully the claims of one group at the expense of committing grave injustice against the other.

3. At its forty-seventh meeting on 27 August 1947, the Committee formally rejected both of the extreme solutions. In taking this action the Committee was fully aware that both Arabs and Jews advance strong claims to rights and interests in Palestine, the Arabs by virtue of being for centuries the indigenous and preponderant people there, and the Jews by virtue of historical association with the country and international pledges made to them respecting their rights in it. But the Committee also realized that the crux of the Palestine problem is to be found in

211

# Annex 1

the fact that two sizeable groups, an Arab population of over 1,200,000 and a Jewish population of over 600,000, with intense nationalist aspirations, are diffused throughout a country that is arid, limited in area, and poor in all essential resources. It was relatively easy to conclude, therefore, that since both groups steadfastly maintain their claims, it is manifestly impossible, in the circumstances, to satisfy fully the claims of both groups, while it is indefensible to accept the full claims of one at the expense of the other.

4. Following the rejection of the extreme solutions in its informal discussions, the Committee devoted its attention to the bi-national State and cantonal proposals. It considered both, but the members who may have been prepared to consider these proposals in principle were not impressed by the workability of either. It was apparent that the bi-national solution, although attractive in some of its aspects, would have little meaning unless provision were made for numerical or political parity between the two population groups, as provided for in the proposal of Dr. J. L. Magnes. This, however, would require the inauguration of complicated mechanical devices which are patently artificial and of dubious practicality.

5. The cantonal solution, under the existing conditions of Arab and Jewish diffusion in Palestine, might easily entail an excessive fragmentation of the governmental process, and in its ultimate result, would be quite unworkable....

## Plan of partition with economic union justification

1. The basic premise underlying the partition proposal is that the claims to Palestine of the Arabs and Jews, both possessing validity, are irreconcilable, and that among all of the solutions advanced, partition will provide the most realistic and practicable settlement, and is the most likely to afford a workable basis for meeting in part the claims and national aspirations of both parties.

2. It is a fact that both of these peoples have their historic roots in Palestine, and that both make vital contributions to the

212

# Annex 1

economic and cultural life of the country. The partition solution takes these considerations fully into account.

3. The basic conflict in Palestine is a clash of two intense nationalisms. Regardless of the historical origins of the conflict, the rights and wrongs of the promises and counter-promises, and the international intervention incident to the Mandate, there are now in Palestine some 650,000 Jews and some 1,200,000 Arabs who are dissimilar in their ways of living and, for the time being, separated by political interests which render difficult full and effective political co-operation among them, whether voluntary or induced by constitutional arrangements.

4. Only by means of partition can these conflicting national aspirations find substantial expression and qualify both peoples to take their places as independent nations in the international community and in the United Nations.

5. The partition solution provides that finality which is a most urgent need in the solution. Every other proposed solution would tend to induce the two parties to seek modification in their favour by means of persistent pressure. The grant of independence to both States, however, would remove the basis for such efforts.

6. Partition is based on a realistic appraisal of the actual Arab–Jewish relations in Palestine. Full political co-operation would be indispensable to the effective functioning of any single-State scheme, such as the federal State proposal, except in those cases which frankly envisage either an Arab- or a Jewish-dominated State.

7. Partition is the only means available by which political and economic responsibility can be placed squarely on both Arabs and Jews, with the prospective result that, confronted with responsibility for bearing fully the consequences of their own actions, a new and important element of political amelioration would be introduced. In the proposed federal-State solution, this factor would be lacking.

8. Jewish immigration is the central issue in Palestine today and is the one factor, above all others, that rules out the necessary co-operation between the Arab and Jewish communities in a single State. The creation of a Jewish State under a partition

scheme is the only hope of removing this issue from the arena of conflict.

9. It is recognized that partition has been strongly opposed by Arabs, but it is felt that that opposition would be lessened by a solution which definitively fixes the extent of territory to be allotted to the Jews with its implicit limitation on immigration. The fact that the solution carries the sanction of the United Nations involves a finality which should allay Arab fears of further expansion of the Jewish State.

10. In view of the limited area and resources of Palestine, it is essential that, to the extent feasible, and consistent with the creation of two independent States, the economic unity of the country should be preserved. The partition proposal, therefore, is a qualified partition, subject to such measures and limitations as are considered essential to the future economic and social well-being of both States. Since the economic self-interest of each State would be vitally involved, it is believed that the minimum measure of economic unity is possible, where that of political unity is not.

11. Such economic unity requires the creation of an economic association by means of a treaty between the two States. The essential objectives of this association would be a common customs system, a common currency and the maintenance of a country-wide system of transport and communications....

# INDEPENDENCE

The following document announcing the official establishment of the State of Israel was signed by David Ben-Gurion
and the members of the Provisional Council of State on 14
May 1948.

## DECLARATION OF THE ESTABLISHMENT OF THE STATE OF ISRAEL*
### 14 May 1948

Eretz-Israel[1] was the birthplace of the Jewish people. Here their
spiritual, religious and political identity was shaped. Here they
first attained to statehood, created cultural values of national and
universal significance and gave to the world the eternal Book of
Books.

After being forcibly exiled from their land the people kept
faith with it throughout their dispersion and never ceased to pray
and hope for their return to it and for the restoration in it of their
political freedom.

Impelled by this historic and traditional attachment, Jews
strove in every successive generation to re-establish themselves
in their ancient homeland. In recent decades they returned in
their masses. Pioneers, Ma'apilim[2] and defenders, they made
deserts bloom, revived the Hebrew language, built villages and
towns, and created a thriving community, controlling its own
economy and culture, loving peace but knowing how to defend
itself, bringing the blessings of progress to all the country's
inhabitants, and aspiring towards independent nationhood.

In the year 5657 (1897), at the summons of the spiritual father

---

* Published in the Official Gazette No 1 of the 5th Iva. 5708 (14 May 1984).
[1] Eretz-Israel (Hebrew)—the Land of Israel, Palestine.
[2] Ma' apilim (Hebrew)—immigrants coming to Eretz-Israel in defiance of
restrictive legislation.

of the Jewish state, Theodor Herzl, the first Zionist congress convened and proclaimed the right of the Jewish people to national rebirth in its own country.

This right was recognized in the Balfour Declaration of the 2nd November, 1917, and re-affirmed in the Mandate of the League of Nations which, in particular, gave international sanction to the historic connection between the Jewish people and Eretz-Israel and to the right of the Jewish people to rebuild its national home.

The catastrophe which recently befell the Jewish people—the massacre of millions of Jews in Europe—was another clear demonstration of the urgency of solving the problem of its homelessness by re-establishing in Eretz-Israel the Jewish state, which would open the gates of the homeland wide to every Jew and confer upon the Jewish people the status of a fully-privileged member of the comity of nations.

Survivors of the Nazi holocaust in Europe, as well as Jews from other parts of the world, continued to migrate to Eretz-Israel, undaunted by difficulties, restrictions and dangers, and never ceased to assert their right to a life of dignity, freedom and honest toil in their national homeland.

In the Second World War, the Jewish community of this country contributed its full share to the struggle of the freedom- and peace-loving nations against the forces of Nazi wickedness and, by the blood of its soldiers and its war effort, gained the right to be reckoned among the peoples who founded the United Nations.

On the 29th November, 1947, the United Nations General Assembly passed a resolution calling for the establishment of a Jewish state in Eretz-Israel. The General Assembly required the inhabitants of Eretz-Israel to take such steps as were necessary on their part for the implementation of that resolution. This recognition by the United Nations of the right of the Jewish people to establish their state is irrevocable.

This right is the natural right of the Jewish people to be masters of their own fate, like all other nations, in their own sovereign state.

Accordingly we, members of the People's Council, represen-

# Annex 2

tatives of the Jewish community of Eretz-Israel and of the Zionist movement, are here assembled on the day of the termination of the British mandate over Eretz-Israel and, by virtue of our natural and historic right and on the strength of the resolution of the United Nations General Assembly, hereby declare the establishment of a Jewish state in Eretz-Israel, to be known as the State of Israel.

We declare that, with effect from the moment of the termination of the mandate, being tonight, the eve of Sabbath, the 6th Iyar, 5708 (15th May, 1948), until the establishment of the elected, regular authorities of the state in accordance with the constitution which shall be adopted by the elected Constituent Assembly not later than the 1st October, 1948, the People's Council shall act as a provisional council of state, and its executive organ, the People's Administration, shall be the provisional government of the Jewish state, to be called "Israel".

The State of Israel will be open for Jewish immigration and for the ingathering of the exiles. It will foster the development of the country for the benefit of all its inhabitants, it will be based on freedom, justice and peace as envisaged by the prophets of Israel, it will ensure complete equality of social and political rights to all its inhabitants irrespective of religion, race or sex, it will guarantee freedom of religion, conscience, language, education and culture, it will safeguard the holy places of all religions, and it will be faithful to the principles of the Charter of the United Nations.

The State of Israel is prepared to co-operate with the agencies and representatives of the United Nations in implementing the resolution of the General Assembly of the 29th November, 1947, and will take steps to bring about the economic union of the whole of Eretz-Israel.

We appeal to the United Nations to assist the Jewish people in the building-up of its state and to receive the State of Israel into the comity of nations.

We appeal—in the very midst of the onslaught launched against us now for months—to the Arab inhabitants of the State of Israel to preserve peace and participate in the upbuilding of the state on the basis of full and equal citizenship and due representation in all its provisional and permanent institutions.

# Annex 2

We extend our hand to all neighbouring states and their peoples in an offer of peace and good neighbourliness, and appeal to them to establish bonds of co-operation and mutual help with the sovereign Jewish people settled in its own land. The State of Israel is prepared to do its share in a common effort for the advancement of the entire Middle East.

We appeal to the Jewish people throughout the diaspora to rally round the Jews of Eretz-Israel in the tasks of immigration and upbuilding and to stand by them in the great struggle for the realization of the age-old dream—the redemption of Israel.

Placing our trust in the Almighty, we affix our signatures to this proclamation at this session of the Provisional Council of State, on the soil of the homeland, in the city of Tel Aviv, on this Sabbath eve, the 5th day of Iyar, 5708 (14th May, 1948).

# CONVENTION

**The following is taken from the text of the Palestine National Covenant, adopted by the PLO in 1964 and amended in 1968.**

**Article 1:** Palestine is the homeland of the Arab Palestinian people; it is an indivisible part of the Arab homeland, and the Palestinian people are an integral part of the Arab nation.

**Article 2:** Palestine, with the boundaries it had during the British Mandate, is an indivisible territorial unit.

**Article 3:** The Palestinian people possess the legal right to their homeland and have the right to determine their destiny after achieving the liberation of their country in accordance with their wishes and entirely of their own accord and will.

**Article 4:** The Palestinian identity is a genuine, essential and inherent characteristic; it is transmitted from parents to children. The Zionist occupation and the dispersal of the Palestinian Arab people, through the disasters which befell them, do not make them lose their Palestinian identity and their membership of the Palestinian community, nor do they negate them.

**Article 5:** The Palestinians are those Arab nationals who, until 1947, normally resided in Palestine regardless of whether they were evicted from it or have stayed there. Anyone born, after that date, of a Palestinian father—whether inside Palestine or outside it—is also a Palestinian.

**Article 6:** The Jews who had normally resided in Palestine until the beginning of the Zionist invasion will be considered Palestinians.

**Article 7:** That there is a Palestinian community and that it has material, spiritual and historical connections with Palestine are

# Annex 3

indisputable facts. It is a national duty to bring up individual Palestinians in an Arab revolutionary manner. All means of information and education must be adopted in order to acquaint the Palestinian with his country in the most profound manner, both spiritual and material, that is possible. He must be prepared for the armed struggle and ready to sacrifice his wealth and his life in order to win back his homeland and bring about its liberation.

**Article 8:** The phase in their history, through which the Palestinian people are now living, is that of national (*watani*) struggle for the liberation of Palestine. Thus the conflicts among the Palestinian national forces are secondary, and should be ended for the sake of the basic conflict that exists between the forces of Zionism and of imperialism on the one hand, and the Palestinian Arab people on the other. On this basis the Palestinian masses, regardless of whether they are residing in the national homeland or in diaspora (*mahajir*) constitute—both their organization and the individuals—one national front working for the retrieval of Palestine and its liberation through armed struggle.

**Article 9:** Armed struggle is the only way to liberate Palestine. Thus it is the overall strategy, not merely a tactical phase. The Palestinian Arab people assert their absolute determination and firm resolution to continue their armed struggle and to work for an armed popular revolution for the liberation of their country and their return to it. They also assert their right to normal life in Palestine and to exercise their right to self-determination and sovereignty over it.

**Article 10:** Commando action constitutes the nucleus of the Palestinian popular liberation war. This requires its escalation, comprehensiveness and mobilization of all the Palestinian popular and educational efforts and their organization and involvement in the armed Palestinian revolution. It also requires the achieving of unity for the national struggle among the different groupings of the Palestinian people, and between the Palestinian people and the Arab masses so as to secure the continuation of the revolution, its escalation and victory.

# Annex 3

**Article 11:** The Palestinians will have three mottoes: national (*wataniyya*) unity, national (*qawmiyya*) mobilization and liberation.

**Article 12:** The Palestinian people believe in Arab unity. In order to contribute their share towards the attainment of that objective, however, they must, at the present stage of their struggle, safeguard their Palestinian identity and develop their consciousness of that identity, and oppose any plan that may dissolve or impair it.

**Article 13:** Arab unity and the liberation of Palestine are two complementary objectives, the attainment of either of which facilitates the attainment of the other. Thus, Arab unity leads to the liberation of Palestine; the liberation of Palestine leads to Arab unity; and work towards the realization of one objective proceeds side by side with work towards the realization of the other.

**Article 14:** The destiny of the Arab nation, and indeed Arab existence itself, depends upon the destiny of the Palestinian cause. From this interdependence springs the Arab nation's pursuit of, and striving for, the liberation of Palestine. The people of Palestine play the role of the vanguard in the realization of this sacred national (*qawmi*) goal.

**Article 15:** The liberation of Palestine, from an Arab viewpoint, is a national duty and it attempts to repel the Zionist and imperialist aggression against the Arab homeland, and aims at the elimination of Zionism in Palestine. Absolute responsibility for this falls upon the Arab nation—peoples and governments—with the Arab people of Palestine in the vanguard.

Accordingly the Arab nation must mobilize all its military, human and moral and spiritual capabilities to participate actively with the Palestinian people in the liberation of Palestine. It must, particularly in the phase of the armed Palestinian revolution, offer and furnish the Palestinian people with all possible help, and material and human support, and make available to them the means and opportunities that will enable them to continue to carry out their leading role in the armed revolution, until they liberate their homeland.

# Annex 3

**Article 16:** The liberation of Palestine, from a spiritual point of view, will provide the Holy Land with an atmosphere of safety and tranquility, which in turn will safeguard the country's religious sanctuaries and guarantee freedom of worship and of visit to all without discrimination of race, colour, language, or religion. Accordingly, the people of Palestine look to all spiritual forces in the world for support.

**Article 17:** The liberation of Palestine, from a human point of view, will restore to the Palestinian individual his dignity, pride and freedom. Accordingly the Palestinian Arab people look forward to the support of all those who believe in the dignity of man and his freedom in the world.

**Article 18:** The liberation of Palestine, from an international point of view, is a defensive action necessitated by the demands of self-defence. Accordingly, the Palestinian people, desirous as they are of the friendship of all people, look to freedom-loving, justice-loving and peace-loving states for support in order to restore their legitimate rights in Palestine, to re-establish peace and security in the country, and to enable its people to exercise national sovereignty and freedom.

**Article 19:** The partition of Palestine in 1947 and the establishment of the State of Israel are entirely illegal, regardless of the passage of time, because they were contrary to the will of the Palestinian people and to their natural right in their homeland, and inconsistent with the principles embodied in the Charter of the United Nations, particularly the right to self-determination.

**Article 20:** The Balfour Declaration, the Mandate for Palestine and everything that has been based upon them, are deemed null and void. Claims of historical or religious ties of Jews with Palestine are incompatible with the facts of history and the true conception of what constitutes statehood. Judaism, being a religion, is not an independent nationality. Nor do Jews constitute a single nation with an identity of its own; they are citizens of the states to which they belong.

**Article 21:** The Arab Palestinian people, expressing themselves by the armed Palestinian revolution, reject all solutions which

# Annex 3

are substitutes for the total liberation of Palestine and reject all proposals aiming at the liquidation of the Palestinian problem, or its internationalization.

**Article 22:** Zionism is a political movement organically associated with international imperialism and antagonistic to all action for liberation and to progressive movements in the world. It is racist and fanatic in its nature, aggressive, expansionist and colonial in its aims, and fascist in its methods. Israel is the instrument of the Zionist movement, and a geographical base for world imperialism placed strategically in the midst of the Arab homeland to combat the hopes of the Arab nation for liberation, unity and progress. Israel is a constant source of threat *vis-a-vis* peace in the Middle East and the whole world. Since the liberation of Palestine will destroy the Zionist and imperialist presence and will contribute to the establishment of peace in the Middle East, the Palestinian people look for the support of all the progressive and peaceful forces and urge them all, irrespective of their affiliations and beliefs, to offer the Palestinian people all aid and support in their just struggle for the liberation of their homeland.

**Article 23:** The demands of security and peace, as well as the demands of right and justice, require all states to consider Zionism an illegitimate movement, to outlaw its existence, and to ban its operations, in order that friendly relations among peoples may be preserved, and the loyalty of citizens to their respective homelands safeguarded.

**Article 24:** The Palestinian people believe in the principles of justice, freedom, sovereignty, self-determination, human dignity, and in the right of all peoples to exercise them.

**Article 25:** For the realization of the goals of this Charter and its principles, the Palestinian Liberation Organization will perform its role in the liberation of Palestine in accordance with the Constitution of this Organization.

**Article 26:** The Palestine Liberation Organization, representative of the Palestinian revolutionary forces, is responsible for the Palestinian Arab people's movement in its struggle—to retrieve

223

its homeland, liberate and return to it and exercise the right to self-determination in it—in all military, political and financial fields and also for whatever may be required by the Palestinian case on the inter-Arab and international levels.

**Article 27:** The Palestinian Liberation Organization shall co-operate with all Arab states, each according to its potentialities; and will adopt a neutral policy among them in the light of the requirements of the war of liberation; and on this basis it shall not interfere in the internal affairs of any Arab State.

**Article 28:** The Palestinian Arab people assert the genuineness and independence of their national (*wataniyya*) revolution and reject all forms of intervention, trusteeship and subordination.

**Article 29:** The Palestinian people possess the fundamental and genuine legal right to liberate and retrieve their homeland. The Palestinian people determine their attitude towards all states and forces on the basis of the stands they adopt *vis-a-vis* the Palestinian case and the extent of the support they offer to the Palestinian revolution to fulfill the aims of the Palestinian people.

**Article 30:** Fighters and carriers of arms in the war of liberation are the nucleus of the popular army which will be the protective force for the gains of the Palestinian Arab people.

**Article 31:** The Organization shall have a flag, an oath of allegiance and an anthem. All this shall be decided upon in accordance with a special regulation.

**Article 32:** Regulations, which shall be known as the Constitution of the Palestine Liberation Organization, shall be annexed to this Charter. It shall lay down the manner in which the Organization, and its organs and institutions, shall be constituted; the respective competence of each; and the requirements of its obligations under the Charter.

**Article 33:** This Charter shall not be amended save by (vote of) a majority of two-thirds of the total membership of the National Congress of the Palestine Liberation Organization (taken) at a special session convened for that purpose.

# RESOLUTIONS

**The following is Security Council Resolution 242, passed on 22 November 1967, after the Six Day War.**

The Security Council,

*Expressing* its continuing concern with the grave situation in the Middle East,

*Emphasizing* the inadmissibility of the acquisition of territory by war and the need to work for a just and lasting peace in which every State in the area can live in security,

*Emphasizing further* that all Member States in their acceptance of the Charter of the United Nations have undertaken a commitment to act in accordance with Article 2 of the Charter,

1. *Affirms* that the fulfilment of Charter principles requires the establishment of a just and lasting peace in the Middle East which should include the application of both the following principles:
    (i) Withdrawal of Israel armed forces from territories occupied in the recent conflict;
    (ii) Termination of all claims or states of belligerency and respect for and acknowledgement of the sovereignty, territorial integrity and political independence of every State in the area and their right to live in peace within secure and recognized boundaries free from threats or acts of force;

2. *Affirms further* the necessity
    (a) For guaranteeing freedom of navigation through international waterways in the area;
    (b) For achieving a just settlement of the refugee problem;
    (c) For guaranteeing the territorial inviolability and political independence of every State in the area, through measures including the establishment of demilitarized zones;

cc-o

# Annex 4

3. *Requests* the Secretary-General to designate a Special Representative to proceed to the Middle East to establish and maintain contacts with the States concerned in order to promote agreement and assist efforts to achieve a peaceful and accepted settlement in accordance with the provisions and principles in this resolution;

4. *Requests* the Secretary-General to report to the Security Council on the progress of the efforts of the Special Representative as soon as possible.

**The following is Security Council Resolution 338, passed on 22 October 1973 during the Yom Kippur War.**

The Security Council

1. Calls upon all parties to the present fighting to cease all firing and terminate all military activity immediately, no later than 12 hours after the moment of the adoption of this decision, in the positions they now occupy;

2. Calls upon the parties concerned to start immediately after the cease-fire the implementation of Security Council Resolution 242 (1967) in all of its parts;

3. Decides that immediately and concurrently with the cease-fire, negotiations start between the parties concerned under appropriate auspices aimed at establishing a just and durable peace in the Middle East.

# CAMP DAVID

The following agreement was signed by the governments of Egypt and Israel and witnessed by the President of the United States in September 1978.

# I. THE CAMP DAVID ACCORDS

## The Framework for Peace in the Middle East

Mohammed Anwar al-Sadat, President of the Arab Republic of Egypt, and Menahem Begin, Prime Minister of Israel, met with Jimmy Carter, President of the United States of America, at Camp David from Sept. 5 to Sept. 17, 1978, and have agreed on the following framework for peace in the Middle East. They invite other parties to the Arab–Israeli conflict to adhere to it:

### PREAMBLE

The search for peace in the Middle East must be guided by the following:

The agreed basis for a peaceful settlement of the conflict between Israel and its neighbours is UN Security Council Resolution 242 in all its parts.

After four wars during 30 years, despite intensive humane efforts, the Middle East, which is the cradle of civilization and the birthplace of three great religions, does not yet enjoy the blessings of peace. The people of the Middle East yearn for peace, so that the vast human and natural resources of the region can be turned to the pursuits of peace and so that this area can become a model for coexistence and cooperation among nations.

The historic initiative by President Sadat in visiting Jerusalem

# Annex 5

and the reception accorded to him by the parliament, government and people of Israel, and the reciprocal visit of Prime Minister Begin to Ismailia, the peace proposals made by both leaders, as well as the warm reception of these missions by the peoples of both countries, have created an unprecedented opportunity for peace which must not be lost if this generation and future generations are to be spared the tragedies of war.

The provisions of the Charter of the United Nations and the other accepted norms of international law and legitimacy now provide accepted standards for the conduct of relations between all states.

To achieve a relationship of peace, in the spirit of Article 2 of the UN Charter, future negotiations between Israel and any neighbour prepared to negotiate peace and security with it, are necessary for the purpose of carrying out all the provisions and principles of Resolutions 242 and 338.

Peace requires respect for the sovereignty, territorial integrity and political independence of every state in the area and their right to live in peace within secure and recognized boundaries free from threats or acts of force. Progress toward that goal can accelerate movement toward a new era of reconciliation in the Middle East marked by cooperation in promoting economic development, in maintaining stability and in assuring security.

Security is enhanced by a relationship of peace and by cooperation between nations which enjoy normal relations. In addition, under the terms of peace treaties, the parties can, on the basis of reciprocity, agree to special security arrangements such as demilitarized zones, limited armaments areas, early warning stations, the presence of international forces, liaison, agreed measures for monitoring, and other arrangements that they agree are useful.

Taking these factors into account, the parties are determined to reach a just, comprehensive, and durable settlement of the Middle East conflict through the conclusion of peace treaties based on Security Council Resolutions 242 and 338 in all their parts. Their purpose is to achieve peace and good neighbourly relations. They recognize that, for peace to endure, it must involve all those who have been most deeply affected by the

228

# Annex 5

conflict. They therefore agree that this framework as appropriate is intended by them to constitute a basis for peace not only between Egypt and Israel, but also between Israel and each of its other neighbours which is prepared to negotiate peace with Israel on this basis.

With that objective in mind, they have agreed to proceed as follows:

## A. West Bank and Gaza

1. Egypt, Israel, Jordan and the representatives of the Palestinian People should participate in negotiations on the resolution of the Palestinian problem in all its aspects. To achieve that objective, negotiations relating to the West Bank and Gaza should proceed in three stages.

(A) Egypt and Israel agree that, in order to ensure a peaceful and orderly transfer of authority, and taking into account the security concerns of all the parties, there should be transitional arrangements for the West Bank and Gaza for a period not exceeding five years. In order to provide full autonomy to the inhabitants, under these arrangements the Israeli military government and its civilian administration will be withdrawn as soon as a self-governing authority has been freely elected by the inhabitants of these areas to replace the existing military government.

To negotiate the details of a transitional arrangement, the government of Jordan will be invited to join the negotiations on the basis of this framework. These new arrangements should give due consideration to both the principle of self-government by the inhabitants of these territories and to the legitimate security concerns of the parties involved.

(B) Egypt, Israel, and Jordan will agree on the modalities for establishing the elected self-governing authority in the West Bank and Gaza. The delegations of Egypt and Jordan may include Palestinians from the West Bank and Gaza or other Palestinians as mutually agreed. The parties will negotiate an agreement which will define the powers and responsibilities of the self-governing authority to be exercised in the West Bank and

229

Gaza. A withdrawal of Israeli armed forces will take place and there will be a redeployment of the remaining Israeli forces into specified security locations.

The agreement will also include arrangements for assuring internal and external security and public order. A strong local police force will be established, which may include Jordanian citizens. In addition, Israeli and Jordanian forces will participate in joint patrols and in the manning of control posts to assure the security of the borders.

(C) When the self-governing authority (administrative council) in the West Bank and Gaza is established and inaugurated, the transitional period of five years will begin. As soon as possible, but not later than the third year after the beginning of the transitional period, negotiations will take place to determine the final status of the West Bank and Gaza and its relationship with its neighbours, and to conclude a peace treaty between Israel and Jordan by the end of the transitional period.

These negotiations will be conducted among Egypt, Israel, Jordan, and the elected representatives of the inhabitants of the West Bank and Gaza. Two separate but related committees will be convened, one committee, consisting of representatives of the four parties which will negotiate and agree on the final status of the West Bank and Gaza, and its relationship with its neighbours, and the second committee, consisting of representatives of Israel and representatives of Jordan to be joined by the elected representatives of the inhabitants of the West Bank and Gaza, to negotiate the peace treaty between Israel and Jordan, taking into account the agreement reached on the final status of the West Bank and Gaza.

The negotiations shall be based on all the provisions and principles of UN Security Council Resolution 242. The negotiations will resolve, among other matters, the location of the boundaries and the nature of the security arrangements.

The solution from the negotiations must also recognize the legitimate rights of the Palestinian people and their just requirements. In this way, the Palestinians will participate in the determination of their own future through:

—1) The negotiations among Egypt, Israel, Jordan and the

# *Annex 5*

representatives of the inhabitants of the West Bank and Gaza to agree on the final status of the West Bank and Gaza and other outstanding issues by the end of the transitional period.

—2) Submitting their agreement to a vote by the elected representatives of the inhabitants of the West Bank and Gaza.

—3) Providing for the elected representatives of the inhabitants of the West Bank and Gaza to decide how they shall govern themselves consistent with the provisions of their agreement.

—4) Participating as stated above in the work of the committee negotiating the peace treaty between Israel and Jordan.

2. All necessary measures will be taken and provisions made to assure the security of Israel and its neighbours during the transitional period and beyond. To assist in providing such security, a strong local police force will be constituted by the self-governing authority. It will be composed of inhabitants of the West Bank and Gaza. The police will maintain continuing liaison on internal security matters with the designated Israeli, Jordanian and Egyptian officers.

3. During the transitional period, the representatives of Egypt, Israel, Jordan and the self-governing authority will constitute a continuing committee to decide by agreement on the modalities of admission of persons displaced from the West Bank and Gaza in 1967, together with necessary measures to prevent disruption and disorder. Other matters of common concern may also be dealt with by this committee.

4. Egypt and Israel will work with each other and with other interested parties to establish agreed procedures for a prompt, just and permanent implementation of the resolution of the refugee problem.

## B. *Egypt–Israel*

1. Egypt and Israel undertake not to resort to the threat or the use of force to settle disputes. Any disputes shall be settled by peaceful means in accordance with the provisions of Article 33 of the Charter of the United Nations.

# Annex 5

2. In order to achieve peace between them, the parties agreed to negotiate in good faith with a goal of concluding within three months from the signing of this Framework a peace treaty between them, while inviting the other parties to the conflict to proceed simultaneously to negotiate and conclude similar peace treaties with a view to achieving a comprehensive peace in the area. The Framework for the conclusion of a peace treaty between Egypt and Israel will govern the peace negotiations between them. The parties will agree on the modalities and the timetable for the implementation of their obligations under the treaty.

## C. Associated Principles

1. Egypt and Israel state that the principles and provisions described below should apply to peace treaties between Israel and each of its neighbours—Egypt, Jordan, Syria and Lebanon.

2. Signatories shall establish among themselves relationships normal to states at peace with one another. To this end, they should undertake to abide by all the provisions of the Charter of the United Nations. Steps to be taken in this respect include:
(A)  Full recognition.
(B)  Abolishing economic boycotts.
(C)  Guaranteeing that under their jurisdiction the citizens of the other parties shall enjoy the protection of the due process of law.

3. Signatories should explore possibilities for economic development in the context of final peace treaties, with the objective of contributing to the atmosphere of peace, cooperation and friendship which is their common goal.

4. Claims commissions may be established for the mutual settlement of all financial claims.

5. The United States shall be invited to participate in the talks on matters related to the modalities of the implementation of the agreements and working out the timetable for the carrying out of the obligations of the parties.

# *Annex 5*

6. The United Nations Security Council shall be requested to endorse the peace treaties and ensure that their provisions shall not be violated. The permanent members of the Security Council shall be requested to underwrite the peace treaties and ensure respect for their provisions. They shall also be requested to conform their policies and actions with the undertakings contained in this framework.

For the Government of the                 For the Government
Arab Republic of Egypt:                   of Israel:


Witnessed by:


Jimmy Carter, President of the United States of America


**The following is an extract from the document which officially terminated the state of war between Israel and Egypt on 26 March 1979.**


## II. THE PEACE TREATY WITH EGYPT


**Treaty of Peace between the Arab Republic of Egypt and the State of Israel**


The Government of the Arab Republic of Egypt and the Government of the State of Israel;

PREAMBLE

Convinced of the urgent necessity of the establishment of a just, comprehensive and lasting peace in the Middle East in accordance with Security Council Resolutions 242 and 338;

233

# Annex 5

Reaffirming their adherence to the "Framework for Peace in the Middle East Agreed at Camp David", dated September 17, 1978;

Noting that the aforementioned Framework as appropriate is intended to constitute a basis for peace not only between Egypt and Israel but also between Israel and each of its other Arab neighbours which is prepared to negotiate peace with it on this basis;

Desiring to bring to an end the state of war between them and to establish a peace in which every state in the area can live in security;

Convinced that the conclusion of a Treaty of Peace between Egypt and Israel is an important step in the search for comprehensive peace in the area and for the attainment of the settlement of the Arab–Israeli conflict in all its aspects;

Inviting the other Arab parties to this dispute to join the peace process with Israel guided by and based on the principles of the aforementioned Framework;

Desiring as well to develop friendly relations and cooperation between themselves in accordance with the United Nations Charter and the principles of international law governing international relations in times of peace;

Agree to the following provisions in the free exercise of their sovereignty, in order to implement the "Framework for the Conclusion of a Peace Treaty Between Egypt and Israel";

## Article I

1. The state of war between the Parties will be terminated and peace will be established between them upon the exchange of instruments of ratification of this Treaty.

2. Israel will withdraw all its armed forces and civilians from the Sinai behind the international boundary between Egypt and mandated Palestine, and Egypt will resume the exercise of its full sovereignty over the Sinai.

3. Upon completion of the interim withdrawal, the Parties will establish normal and friendly relations.

# Annex 5

## Article II

The permanent boundary between Egypt and Israel is the recognized international boundary between Egypt and the former mandated territory of Palestine, without prejudice to the issue of the status of the Gaza Strip. The Parties recognize this boundary as inviolable. Each will respect the territorial integrity of the other, including their territorial waters and airspace.

## ANNEX 6

**CITIES**

| | |
|---|---:|
| New York | 2,216,000 |
| Los Angeles | 604,000 |
| Jerusalem | 336,000 |
| Tel Aviv | 310,000 |
| Philadelphia | 309,000 |
| Paris | 300,000 |
| Chicago | 254,000 |
| London | 250,000 |
| Moscow | 250,000 |
| Buenos Aires | 180,000 |

**AMERICA**

| | |
|---|---:|
| United States | 5,700,000 |
| Canada | 310,000 |
| Argentina | 228,000 |
| Brazil | 100,000 |
| Others | 130,000 |

236

# Annex 6

## THE JEWISH POPULATION THROUGHOUT THE WORLD

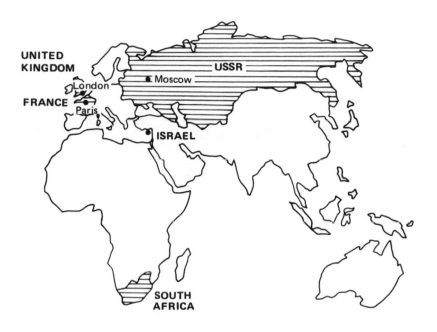

### EUROPE

| | |
|---|---|
| USSR | 1,576,000 |
| France | 530,000 |
| Great Britain | 330,000 |
| West Germany | 33,000 |
| Italy | 32,000 |
| Belgium | 32,000 |
| Rumania | 26,000 |
| Austria | 6,500 |
| Poland | 4,800 |
| | |
| Others | 190,000 |

### ASIA, MIDDLE EAST

| | |
|---|---|
| Israel | 3,561,000 |
| Turkey | 20,000 |
| India | 4,300 |
| Japan | 1,000 |
| | |
| Others | 12,500 |

### AFRICA

| | |
|---|---|
| South Africa | 118,000 |
| Morocco | 13,000 |
| Tunisia | 3,500 |
| | |
| Others | 13,000 |